Recent Research in Psychology

Kevin Lanning

Consistency, Scalability, and Personality Measurement

Springer-Verlag
New York Berlin Heidelberg London
Paris Tokyo Hong Kong Barcelona

Kevin Lanning
Department of Psychology
Oregon State University
Corvallis, Oregon 97331-5303

Library of Congress Cataloging-in-Publication Data
Lanning, Kevin.
Consistency, scalability, and personality measurement / Kevin Lanning.
p. cm. — (Recent research in psychology)
Revision of the author's thesis (doctoral—University of California, Berkeley, 1986).
Includes bibliographical references and index.
1. Personality—Research—Statistical methods. 2. Personality tests. 3. Personality. I. Title. II. Series.
BF698.4.L32 1991
155.2'072—dc20 90-45531

Printed on acid-free paper.

Camera-ready copy provided by the author.
Printed and bound by Edwards Brothers, Inc., Ann Arbor, Michigan.
Printed in the United States of America.

9 8 7 6 5 4 3 2 1

ISBN 0-387-97438-5 Springer-Verlag New York Berlin Heidelberg
ISBN 3-540-97438-5 Springer-Verlag Berlin Heidelberg New York

Preface

Anyone who has taught an introductory level personality course will recognize that there is a yawning gap between "personality theory" and "personality research." This gap between theory and research is disconcerting, even tension-inducing. One way of resolving this tension is by treating the two areas as simply incommensurate, for example, by considering "personality theories" as part of a liberal arts curriculum, with no more (and no less) relevance for a science of personality than Shakespeare or the Magna Carta. This position does have some benefits: The disregard of knotty theoretical issues allows the investigator to respond flexibly to the current *Zeitgeist*, to measure culturally "hot" topics such as *androgyny*, *Type A personality* and *self-monitoring*. But there is also a cost to this timeliness, and that is an insufficient cumulativeness in the field.

One need not abandon personality theory in order to undertake personality research. There is another approach, and that is to attempt to bridge the gap between theory and research by, on the one hand, re-expressing theoretical concepts in a measurable form and, on the other, by re-examining personality research in light of these personality theories.

In the first chapter of this book, I examine the theoretical (or, more accurately, metatheoretical) concept of *trait*. The concept of trait in traditional (e.g., Allportian) personality theory is shown to be quite different from the concept as it is used in contemporary personality research. Proper measurement of traits requires a conceptually sound index of consistency, and in Chapter 2, I propose that individual differences in scalability provide such an index. In Chapter 3, I examine some expected relations between scalability scores and traditional "elevation" measures of traits. In the remaining chapters, I present a series of empirical investigations. The first of these, in Chapter 4, assesses individual differences in scalability for the trait of hostility on a small sample of subjects seen in an in-depth assessment at the Institute of Personality Assessment and Research (IPAR). The second describes a larger scale multivariate investigation, using a naturalistic situation-behavior inventory (Chapters 5 and 6). The third study, in Chapter 7, assesses individual differences in scalability on two personality inventories, the California Psychological Inventory (CPI; Gough, 1987) and the Multidimensional Personality Questionnaire (Tellegen, 1982). In concluding, I re-examine the metatheoretical arguments of the first chapter in light of the subsequent empiricism. This leads to a reassessment of my methods as well as an additional empirical study, in which individual differences in authoritarianism are examined.

This book is a revision of my doctoral dissertation, filed in 1986 at the University of California, Berkeley. The last two chapters have been entirely rewritten. Elsewhere, changes are more modest, but I have attempted to cite recent references where appropriate and to clarify my arguments throughout.

A number of acknowledgements are in order. Although it would be impossible to explicitly thank all of those who made this work possible, I do want to mention the critical contribution of the research participants, both in Berkeley and in Corvallis. My dissertation benefitted from the feedback of Ravenna Helson, Barbara Mellers and my committee members, Harrison Gough, William MacKinley Runyan, and Jack Block (chairman).

The initial empirical investigations (Chapter 4) were supported by a National Science Foundation graduate fellowship. Dr. John Kamp kindly shared the Multidimensional Personality Questionnaire (MPQ) data described in Chapter 7. The study of the California Psychological Inventory (CPI) described in Chapter 7, as well as the analyses of the CPI and MPQ data, was supported by National Institute of Health Biomedical Grant RR7079. A preliminary version of the analyses presented in Chapter 7 was presented at the 1988 meeting of the American Psychological Association in Atlanta. Additional analyses of the data in Chapter 6 have previously appeared in the *Journal of Personality and Social Psychology* (Lanning, 1988). The study of authoritarianism described in Chapter 8 was funded by a grant from the Harry Frank Guggenheim foundation.

Four years ago, I dedicated my dissertation to my wife Carol, "for her continuing compassion and humor." I could not write a more accurate appreciation today; she is beautiful testimony to the consistency of personality.

K. L.

Contents

1

Personality Traits and Psychological Explanation

The central concept of personality psychology is the trait. Yet there is little consensus in the field concerning the definition of traits. Most investigators would agree that personality traits are relatively enduring psychological characteristics of persons, and that traits function, either validly or invalidly, to describe, predict, explain, or understand persons and their behavior. But this definition is quite broad, and beyond it there is little consensus. Investigators appear to disagree about virtually every feature of personality traits. Disagreements occur on such basic issues as the location of traits (whether in the head of the actor or in the language of the observer), the origins of traits (genetic *versus* environmental contributions, early *versus* recent experience), the plasticity of traits in response to environmental change, and the importance of traits *vis-a-vis* other aspects of personality, the proximal environment, and the sociocultural context (e.g., Allport, 1966; Buss & Craik, 1985; Cattell, 1946; Feshbach & Weiner, 1986; Guilford, 1975; Hirschberg, 1978; Kluckhohn & Murray, 1961; Runyan, 1982; Wiggins, 1974).

This lack of consensus would be acceptable, and perhaps even fruitful, if investigators were routinely explicit in citing their conception of trait. Unfortunately, this qualification is rarely met: Golding (1978) has estimated that over 90% of the uses of *trait* in the empirical literature do not define the term. This history of ambiguity assures that unmodified use of *trait* will carry unknown and differing implications to different readers. As a direct result of this excesss baggage, some more careful writers prefer to avoid use of the term altogether (e.g., Block & Block, 1980; Gough, 1987).

Although the ambiguity of the trait concept is problematic, the diversity of ideas which it masks is not (see also Kenrick & Funder, 1988). That is, an examination of different conceptions of "trait" can, in principle, lead to the recognition of basic issues that might otherwise be obscured. In this first chapter, I articulate some different conceptions of traits. Two core positions are distinguished. Adherents of the first position consider traits to be veritable psychological structures; adherents of the second position argue that these variables are, instead, mere constructions of society. The two positions differ most clearly in their views regarding the explanatory value of traits; accordingly, I will consider the role of personality traits in explanation at some length. The chapter concludes with a discussion of the implications of my arguments, particularly with regard to the role of consistency in personality theory and measurement.

1.1 Personality traits as psychological structures

Among those psychologists who argue that personality traits exist as veritable psychological structures, two approaches can be discerned. The first of these is the idiographic or "individual structural" position. The second is the nomothetic or "common structural" position. I will consider each in turn.

1.1.1 Allport and the individual structural position

The most prominent advocate of the structural position is Gordon Allport. Over fifty years ago, Allport defined trait as

> ... a generalized and focalized neuropsychic system (peculiar to the individual), with the capacity to render many stimuli functionally equivalent, and to initiate and guide consistent (equivalent) forms of adaptive and expressive behavior (1937, p. 295).

Each aspect of Allport's position can be rephrased in contemporary terms. The "system" that Allport spoke of may be described as a set of control mechanisms which select, bias, or weigh information in accordance with a particular principle or set of principles. These mechanisms are "neuropsychic"; if we accept materialism as a working premise, no alternative to this seems as likely. Finally, the soundness of the notion that traits "render many stimuli functionally equivalent" follows from the additional recognition that, while each situation or stimulus is different, the perceiver encounters these situations with a relatively finite set of objectives.

Just as Allport's prime concern was with individual differences in behavior, so Kelly (1963) argued that individual differences in perceptual strategies, or *personal constructs*, were crucial in arriving at an understanding of the person. Among mainstream personality psychologists, Kelly's work has often been interpreted as having implications for lay assessment and the psychology of the perceiver (e.g., Mischel, 1968). However, the *constructs* of the lay observer are fully as real as Allport's *traits*. Consequently, Kelly's position may profitably be understood as a variant on the structural approach. It is true that Kelly emphasized "perception" and Allport emphasized "behavior", however, on close examination, the distinction between perception and behavior breaks down (Erdelyi, 1974). For these and other reasons the distinction between constructs and traits is more apparent than real (Allport, 1966).

Many recent empirical investigations have assessed the utility of the individual structural approach. Markus and her colleagues (Markus, 1977; Markus, Crane, Bernstein, & Siladi, 1982; Markus, Smith, & Moreland, 1985; see also S. L. Bem, 1981) have examined the position that salient personality variables may be interpreted as cognitive schemas (structures) which guide perception. Person-centered approaches to personality, such as the life history approach (Runyan, 1982), are the most prominent exemplars of the idiographic position in which the traits used to characterize a person are determined by the person measured rather than by an *a priori* theory or measurement model (Allport, 1965). Working from the premise that empirical consistency implies an underlying psychological structure, both Bem and Kenrick have investigated the utility of distinguishing between consistent and inconsistent individuals (Bem & Allen, 1974; Kenrick & Stringfield, 1980). This premise lies at the core of most contemporary studies of individual differences in personality consistency, including those to be described in the chapters ahead.

1.1.2 The common structural position

A second structural position can be described. Traits are physiological entities, but these physiological structures are essentially similar, or comparable, in all people. Eysenck (1969) is the most prominent advocate of this position. Strelau (1983), like Eysenck a neo-Pavlovian, contends that our common biological endowment gives rise to common psychological parameters such as persistence and speed of reaction; these formal parameters are dimensions of temperament. More content-laden interpretations of temperament have been proposed by A. H. Buss and Plomin (1975) and Conley (1985). Although these investigators differ in the particular traits which they feel describe this domain, all appear to agree that individual differences in dimensions of temperament are highly heritable (A. H. Buss & Plomin, 1975; Conley, 1985; Eysenck, 1969; Strelau, 1985).

Cattell's notion of source trait is similar to this common structural position. Cattell's "dynamic trait structures" describe "... potentialities to respond when certain situations occur, and to do so within limits set by ability and temperament endowments." (1983, p. 201). For Cattell (1946), not all traits are dynamic: Some, for example, are molded by the environment, while still others are constitutional (having to do with temperament), merely semantic, and so forth. Cattell recognizes the existence of individual as well as common traits, and in fact recognizes that "All traits are, in some sense, unique" (1946, p. 61). Factor analysis of a matrix of correlations between variables over persons can only determine the relations between traits in a hypothetical average person, and not the psychological structure of any one individual. Guilford, a major proponent of the technique, explicitly recognized this limitation:

> ... the degree of generality that is found for a trait by factor analysis is a feature of the average person in the group, not necessarily a description of how one person's traits are organized. (1975, p. 813)

Factor analysis serves as a mechanism for discovering personality structure only to the extent that this structure is comparable across individuals. Although the assumption of comparable structure appears justified for certain aspects of personality (i.e., temperament), it is restrictive to argue that the domain of personality is fully represented by the five factors which typically underlie matrices of observer-based trait ratings (Lanning & Gough, 1990; cf., e.g., Digman & Inouye, 1986; Tupes & Christal, 1961).

1.2 Personality traits as psychological constructs

Most contemporary investigators embrace a variant of an alternative interpretation, arguing that traits are social, not physiological entities. In its weak form, the position states that although traits are social in origin, they may nonetheless be used in accurate descriptions of a person's social stimulus value, or in statistical predictions of various real-world outcomes. Several variants of this position can be distinguished: A sociological orientation, a pragmatic orientation, and a behavioral approach. These positions, and the strong constructive position (which argues that traits simply mislead the observer) are presented below.

1.2.1 The weak constructive positions

The sociological position. The scales of Gough's California Psychological Inventory (CPI; Gough, 1987) seek to measure folk concepts; folk concepts are significant because of their broad social relevance. Concepts such as *Dominance* and *Socialization* appear across societies and cultures; their significance is therefore pan-cultural rather than culture-specific. In characterizing the CPI, Gough eschews the trait (i.e., structural) model. Gough argues that because dimensions tapped by the CPI are defined by social rather than biological criteria, an extreme score on a dimension does not necessarily imply the presence of a particular physiological substructure. Rather, the score implies that the person is likely to be described in a specifiable way, and that the person is likely to exhibit a characteristic manner of interpersonal behavior. Though the origin of differentiating qualities remains of interest, the mechanism which underlies predictability is less crucial than the pragmatic utility attained through a particular measurement approach (but see Gough, 1971). This pragmatism is shared by each of two other variants on the weak constructive position.

The pragmatic position. A memorable summary of this approach was provided by Guilford: "A trait is any distinguishable, relatively enduring way in which one individual differs from others" (1959, p. 6). Murphy (1947) presented a similar definition. The main emphasis here is on measurement; the ontological status of traits (i.e., as neuropsychic or social entities) is seen as less relevant. The distinction between this position and the individual structural approach has been noted by a number of investigators. The emphasis on measurement has allowed adherents of this position to avoid metatheoretical issues, arguing that the use of test scores does not depend upon a structural approach to personality traits (Hogan, deSoto, & Solano, 1977; Tryon, 1979).

The behavioral position. Several recent discussions of traits have centered on the idea that traits can best be understood as summaries or categories of behavior. The attribution of a trait to a person follows from this:

> Traits are categories for actions and, since actions by definition require actors, traits are used to describe the people who produce the actions as well as the actions themselves. (Hampson, 1982a, p. 3).

Investigators who maintain the behavioral position have been among the most explicit in recent years to cite their definition of trait or disposition (Buss & Craik, 1983; Wiggins, 1974). A trait is, or should be, assigned to a person if that person exhibits a sufficient number of behaviors deemed relevant (i.e., typical or prototypical) for that trait category. Relevance is normatively determined. Consequently, traits or personality dispositions do not refer to neurological structures, but to "... sociocultural products held by members of a culture" (Buss & Craik, 1983, p. 111; see also Wiggins, 1974). When a person is described as *dominant*, this means simply that he or she has been observed to behave in a dominant fashion over a sufficient number of events.

Two components of the behavioral position may be delineated. First is the ontological position that traits are social constructions (Buss & Craik, 1983). Second is the measurement approach under which scores on a personality trait are assigned as a function of the frequency of a set of prototypical behaviors (e.g., Buss & Craik, 1980). The two components should be considered as separate: The summary approach to measurement is consistent with a structural position in which multiple generating processes underlie topographically similar behaviors. Further, where error of measurement is important, considerations of statistical power may render the summary approach appropriate, regardless of the ontological stance of the investigator.

Under this behavioral approach, traits arise from, and are coterminous with, entirely observable events. Because this position does not hypothesize covert events, it can be characterized as positivistic, sharing with Skinner (1953) the conviction that traits are not causes, but summaries of behavior. Though traits cannot explain behavior, they can provide valid summaries or descriptions of behavior. Further, because what has happened in the past is likely to recur, traits defined in this way can serve as valid predictors of future behavior.

Although this perspective sees traits as constructions, traits are nonetheless real. Hampson (1982a) states that "beliefs about trait relations ... are not fictitious, but have a basis in reality" (p. 9). This "basis in reality" is, however, not a physiological structure but a set of social rules. Traits are social, not structural: Buss and Craik (1983, p. 118) discuss the disposition to be "aversive" and Hampson (1983, p. 402) has examined the trait of "irritating". Both of these dimensions clearly refer more to the social stimulus value of the person as perceived by the observer than to any root quality of the person assessed. Fiske (1974) has similarly emphasized the role of the perceiver in personality assessment.

1.2.2 The strong constructive position

The last interpretation of traits to be considered is the strong constructive position, in which traits are viewed as misattributions (Mischel, 1968; Shweder, 1982). Personality traits lie wholly in the observer, and are merely imposed upon the actor. Traits function merely to organize reality, to give structure to the world, and to assign responsibility for behavior (Nisbett & Ross, 1980); in serving these functions, traits distort and falsify the veridical perception of individuals. This position has been criticized on conceptual, methodological, and empirical grounds (e.g., Alker, 1972; Block, Weiss, & Thorne, 1979; Endler & Magnusson, 1976; Epstein, 1979; Kenrick & Funder, 1988; Magnusson & Endler, 1977); further, its most prominent adherent has since largely recanted (Mischel, 1973, 1985). As, finally, the position is largely negative (by which I mean "unconstructive"), and offers little in the way of theoretical promise, it will not be considered further.

1.3 Structures *versus* constructs

Figure 1.1 depicts a conceptual clustering of the different views of personality traits just introduced. The broadest distinction is that between structural and constructed views of personality. This distinction has been drawn previously, as in Allport's (1937) contrast between *biophysical* and *biosocial* approaches to traits. MacCorquodale and Meehl (1948) and Cronbach and Meehl (1955) used the term "construct" to describe what is here being called structure; this is unfortunate because, as Loevinger (1957) pointed out in her discussion of construct validity,

> *Construct* connotes construction and artifice; yet what is at issue is validity with respect to exactly what the psychologist does not construct:

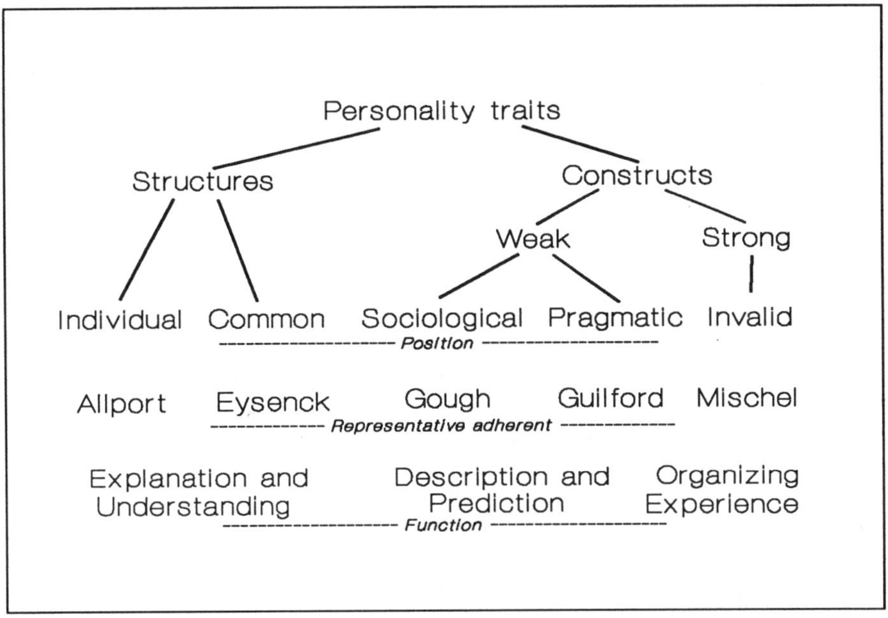

Figure 1.1: Some conceptions of personality traits.

> the validity of the test as a measure of traits which exist prior to and independently of the psychologist's act of measuring. (p. 83)

The distinction between constructs and structures is, in part, metatheoretical. The preference for a structural or constructive orientation is a basic theoretical decision which is largely a product of an investigator's world view; this preference guides the investigators design of research as well as his or her interpretation of empirical data. Averill (1973) noted the parallel between the present structure-construct distinction and the distinction between *Platonism* (in which qualities of value such as goodness and beauty are held to be properties which exist independently of the perceiver) and *Idealism* (in which the sense data which give rise to the notion of value are not considered as derivative from any objective reality, and therefore reside in the perceiver). When the constructive position is combined with the broader position of philosophical idealism, the attribution of traits is as fully valid as the attribution of other qualities. Indeed, "Assigning traits to people is part of a larger process of the social construction of reality." (Hogan, 1983, p. 59).

The word "trait" has been used to characterize both the structural and constructive positions. Ambiguity concerning the meaning of "trait" is not new: The following two definitions of trait date from the 16th and the 18th centuries, respectively.

> Something penned; a line, passage or piece of writing...[*versus*]
> A particular feature of mind or character; a distinguishing quality; a characteristic (*Oxford English Dictionary*, 1971, p. 3375)

The distinction between these two historical definitions is quite similar to that between the modern constructive and structural positions. The historical uses, like the modern positions, are not mutually exclusive - the presence of "something penned" does not invalidate the notion that there is a "feature" underlying the representation.

The constructive position emphasizes that we are always working with constructs: Hampson stresses that "... the human observer does not have direct access to reality" (Hampson, 1982b, p. 170). The structural position accepts this argument, while maintaining that constructs cannot stand alone:

> It is true that psychologists never know traits directly but only through the glass of their constructs, but the data to be judged are manifestations of traits, not manifestations of constructs. (Loevinger, 1957, p. 83)

Murray (Murray et al., 1938) also argued that there was something beyond our constructs: "A need is a construct ... which stands for a force ... in the brain" (p. 123-124).

The structural position recognizes that we are always working with constructs or trait words, but argues that there is something beyond this as well. This "something beyond" leads the structural position to maintain a stronger position concerning the potential informativeness of traits. From the standpoint of the observer, traits are uninformative on the strong constructive position, and progressively increase in their potential informativeness as one moves through the weak constructive positions to the structural positions represented by Eysenck and, finally, Allport.

1.4 Models of explanation

The fundamental distinction between the structural and the constructive positions is in their views regarding the function of traits. According to the structural position, traits can explain behavior (Allport, 1937, 1966). According to the constructive position, traits can only describe or predict behavior (Buss & Craik, 1983; Wiggins, 1974). If traits can explain behavior, then the structural perspective is at least partially sound. In order to evaluate the soundness of the structural position, it is necessary to explicitly consider what is meant by *explanation*.

1.4.1 The covering law model

The received view of explanation is the covering law theory. This position argues that an event is explained by subsuming it under one or more general laws, and then citing the instantiating conditions which rendered the law applicable (Kim, 1967). The structure of an explanation is a logical argument, which may be either demonstrative (the *Deductive-Nomological* model) or probabilistic (the *Inductive-Statistical* model). Because explanation takes the form of a logical argument, a symmetry exists between explanation and prediction. Although in prediction we work forwards from premises to conclusion and in explanation backwards from conclusion to premises, both explanatory and predictive arguments may be represented by structurally identical syllogisms. Consider an abbreviated example, in which we seek to explain or predict John's delinquency (conclusion) from test scores and base rates (premises):

People scoring less than 25 on the CPI Socialization scale are highly likely to be classified as delinquents
John scored less than 25 on CPI Socialization.

-> *John was (is highly likely to be) classified as a delinquent.*

Although the first premise is not a "law of nature", it has achieved suitable empirical validation in a number of studies so that it can safely be called a statistical law (see, e.g., Gough, 1960, 1965; Megargee, 1972). Indeed, there seems to be no question concerning the predictive validity of measures of personality traits such as CPI Socialization. Even the most vocal advocates of the strong constructive position are now recognizing that personality traits can aid in prediction (e.g., Mischel, 1985). Since predictions and explanations are, on this approach, equivalent, it follows that as traits can predict behavior, they therefore can explain behavior as well (Hogan et al., 1977).

1.4.2 The statistical relevance model

Under the covering law theory, the validity of an explanation rests upon the explanation's inclusion of all relevant information (Kim, 1967). The covering law theory does not, however, require that *only* relevant information be included, as in the following syllogism from Salmon (1984):

Whenever John says "Abracadabra" and places salt in water, the salt dissolves.
John said "Abracadabra" and placed the salt in water.

-> *The salt dissolved.*

Salmon's statistical relevance notion of explanation is an extension of the covering law model which specifically excludes non-relevant premises (*John says "Abracadabra"*) from an explanation. For Salmon (1984), the empirical likelihood of the event in question (John's delinquency, the salt dissolving) is examined in each cell of a matrix of potentially relevant variables. A variable is statistically relevant if the probability of the event (salt dissolving) varies in light of the score on this variable (*Abracadabra* versus *no Abracadabra*). Some conceptual difficulties encountered by this approach have been noted elsewhere (Cohen, 1977; Lanning, 1987). For the present purposes, it suffices to note that, because trait scores are statistically related to real world outcomes, traits are potentially explanatory on this extension of the covering law model.

1.4.3 Explanation as non-tautological characterization

On each of these positions, personality traits can explain behavior. But the notion of explanation invoked by these positivistic accounts is pallid and unsatisfying. Is explanation really equivalent to prediction? If so, then we can follow Hogan's pragmatic route (Hogan et al. 1977), and continue to use personality test scores without being concerned about ontology.

But these interpretations of "explanation" have been incomplete. Explanation differs from prediction in that explanation is more informative than prediction. In asking the question "*Why did John watch television*?" we are informing the listener both that we know that the event in question (watching television) did transpire, and, further, that we do not believe that our present knowledge accounts for this event. The listener provides us with an explanation if and only if he or she tells us something which resolves our uncertainty. To achieve this, the explanation must include information that is new, as well as true and relevant.

Consider the following example (Averill, 1973):

A Boeing 747 fell into the Potomac shortly after lift-off.

On the covering law and statistical relevance approaches, we would be forced to accept the following explanation as legitimate:

The plane fell because it was made of metal, and metal is heavier than air.

We reject this explanation because it tells us only something of which we were already aware, while failing to provide new information which would render the event explicable. Averill shares the view of C. Taylor (1970) that a characterization of an event is an explanation if and only if it subsumes the (otherwise incomprehensible) event in question under the normal course of events.

An explanation renders the incomprehensible comprehensible, and achieves this by supplying new information. It follows that if personality traits do not supply new information, then they cannot explain behavior (Buss & Craik, 1983; Skinner, 1953; Wiggins, 1974). Conversely, if traits are informative as well as predictive, then they can explain behavior.

1.5 How traits can explain behavior

When a trait inferred from prior behavior (at time 1) is used to characterize a subsequent event (at time 2), use of the trait term in a characterization has at least weakly explanatory value. Consequently, traits are *not* inherently tautological. This seems unambiguous, although it contradicts the position of a number of investigators (e.g., Buss & Craik, 1983; Mischel, 1968; Wiggins, 1974). I want to make a still stronger argument here: A trait inferred from a sample of behavior (at time 1) may be used to explain instances of that same behavior (again at time 1).

Personality assessment is an exercise in concept formation (Bem, 1983). Necessary processes in concept formation include the negation of hypotheses as well as the summation of common features (Bruner, Goodnow, & Austin, 1954). In personality measurement, processes of negation can provide insights missed by simple summary approaches (see also Lamiell, 1982). As John Stuart Mill pointed out well over a century ago, the application of basic deductive inferences can lead out of tautology, and to new understanding (Mill, 1879). I do not mean to imply that ratiocination is the only manner by which a concept is attained or a problem is solved (Wertheimer, 1945): It is difficult to imagine how the process of intuition or the achievement of empathic understanding could be reduced to simple reason (Allport, 1937). But systematic, reasoned assessment can be quite powerful, and can lead to a characterization of human behavior in terms of explanatory personality structures rather than simply descriptive personality constructs.

A clinician might observe, for example, that a client is frequently anxious. The clinician notes the following events during which Jane manifests anxiety:

Jane feels nervous while taking the subway to work.

Jane cries while waiting at home for her husband.

Because assessment does not end with summation, the clinician notes "non-anxious" events as well:

Jane has a pleasant conversation with a friend as they drive to work together.

Jane sits and reads at home with her husband in the next room.

Following observation of an extensive set of events such as these, the clinician can subtract those elements of Jane's "non-anxious" events which are shared with Jane's "anxious" events. This process of abstraction, by eliminating non-salient situational antecedents, leads to new insights (Lanning, 1986b). In the present case, it emerges that Jane's anxiety is most likely to occur when she is either in a crowd or unexpectedly alone. A label exists for this pattern - we can characterize an aspect of Jane's own personality structure with the descriptive category *agoraphobic* (American Psychiatric Association, 1980). But the statement "Jane stayed home because she is agoraphobic" is more than a mere description, for it avoids tautology and eliminates, or at least renders less probable, competing alternative explanations of her behavior (Hirschberg, 1978).

It is true that a simple summary of behavior which largely ignores non-instances and situational parameters cannot lead to an explanation of concurrent behavior. But this does not imply that such an explanation cannot be derived with more careful observation. Consequently, personality assessment should not be restricted to the simple summation of events.

1.5.1 The role of causality

Before accepting the conclusions that personality structures determine behavior, and that personality traits describe personality structures, one additional aspect of explanation remains to be considered. In a recent discussion of explanation, Salmon (1984) argues that an explanation is more than just a list of statistically relevant variables; these variables must, in addition, be causally linked to the event in question. Salmon's recognition of the role of causality in explanation marks an important departure from the positivist position. When the notion of causality is added to explanation, an explanatory role for personality traits would imply a causal mechanism, an Allportian notion of determining structure.

But what is meant by causality? Although the answer is by no means unequivocal, we can, for the present purposes, consider a variant of what Salmon (1984) has characterized as the "standard" position, on which "cause" can be defined as follows:

> That set of conditions, among all the conditions that occurred, each of which was necessary and the totality of which was sufficient for the occurrence of the event in question. (R. Taylor, 1967, p. 63).

When a naive observer asks, for example, why Jane chose to stay home rather than attend a party which promised to be large and raucous, it is difficult to imagine how personality traits could be excluded from a satisfactory causal explanation (Eysenck, 1970). In the present example, an abbreviated explanation might be along the following lines:

Agoraphobics avoid large and raucous parties.
Jane was and is agoraphobic.
The party was large and raucous.

- > *Jane did not attend the party.*

Here, among the antecedent conditions, Jane's agoraphobia and the raucous nature of the party are individually necessary and jointly sufficient for Jane to remain at home. Such an explanation can meet all of the previously specified requirements for explanation, i.e., it is informative, valid, and statistically relevant.

Causal explanations of behavior. It is useful to consider some of the features of the causal explanations of the type that we have been considering. First, these explanations emerge from the joint presence of both "person" and "situation." Second, these explanations are contemporaneous rather than historical (Allport, 1937; Lewin, 1951; R. Taylor, 1967). Third, explanation is not teleological, but is in terms of "efficient cause." Finally, fourth, the explanation may be described as "shallow" (C. Taylor, 1970): One could readily imagine more profound explanations at varying levels of analysis, which, nonetheless, may be fully consistent with the present explanation.

The last two points require further discussion. On the present analysis, traits - as opposed to needs (Murray et al., 1938) or goals (Schank & Abelson, 1977; Pervin, 1983) - are non-teleological. A trait term describes a particular way of seeing and responding to the world, and not a motivational structure *per se*. It is possible that explanation can be rendered more satisfactory by including concepts such as "goals" and "motives" (Pervin, 1983); however, it should be recognized that explanation in terms of such personality structures may not be irreducibly teleological. (The apparently purposeful behavior of a guided missile or a thermostat, for example, can be best explained without reference to teleology).

The notion that traits function in some sense as "efficient causes" of behavior is not inconsistent with the notion that explanation could ultimately be expressed in neuropsychic terms. Personality traits are dispositions: Quine (1974) has argued that a statement about a disposition is a statement about a physical state or mechanism which the speaker either does not yet fully understand or, for the sake of expediency, chooses to describe in only shorthand terms. (The notion of "expediency" is consistent with the position that personality dispositions might provide a coherent explanation where a neurological description would be incomprehensible or chaotic). Just as *solubility* (the disposition to dissolve in water) characterizes a particular molecular property of a substance, so *agoraphobia* (the disposition to become anxious in crowds, etc.) is a characterization of a particular neuropsychic structure. For Quine, a disposition implies more than simply a statement of contingency, but describes also the structural property which accounts for or generates this contingency. It is in this sense that personality traits are dispositions (Hirschberg, 1978): Personality dispositions describe structures, and are more than simple statements of behavioral contingency. This position is at odds with the popular characterization of dispositions, which sees these as limited to summary statements of behavior (Buss & Craik, 1983; Wiggins, 1974).

1.6 Implications

On each of the criteria cited in the previous paragraphs, personality traits have been shown to have the potential to provide an explanatory account of behavior. Because traits can explain behavior, the structural position is valid. That is, for at least some trait words, there are corresponding personality structures. This is not to say that all trait words represent personality structures. A large class of personality characteristic terms - such as *provincial, deviant,* and *silly* - appear to be descriptive categories which reflect properties of language, culture, and observers rather than properties of actors. These trait words fit the constructive or biosocial model, and will be informative regarding the personality rating process, but not regarding the personality structure of persons rated.

The constructive approach is allied with a particularly powerful measurement model. Further, we are always working with constructs (Loevinger, 1957), and most contemporary investigators have been careful to avoid the structural position. Given these considerations, it would be inappropriate to embrace the structural position without first demonstrating its utility, or rather potential utility. In spite of the conceptual soundness of the structural position, it is important to consider what benefits (if any) are associated with a structural approach to personality measurement.

1.6.1 Assessment as a mapping process

A consequence of recognizing that personality structures exist within the person rated, and personality constructs exist outside of the person rated, is that personality assessment is seen as a mapping process. Analyses of the properties of trait words, whether driven by theoretical concerns (Goldberg, 1982; John, 1986) or empirical ones (Digman & Inouye, 1986; Norman, 1963; Tupes & Christal, 1961) keep us within the domain of cartography. The insight gained into the person by this approach can be no more profound than the anthropological speculations of the armchair tourist.

There is more to personality than the properties of trait words, and it is both possible and advisable to concern ourselves more directly with the underlying geography which gives significance to the map of trait-descriptive terms. One way of doing this is by attempting to more explicitly quantify the goodness-of-fit of trait words to individuals. The "fit" of a trait word to an individual provides an index of the relevance or salience of the trait word for the individual.

Assessment of fit can only take place in a common domain; this common domain is the domain of empirical events, or behaviors in situations. The truth value of a statement concerning fit can be ascertained only after three conditions are satisfied. First, a working definition of the trait word must exist. Second, appropriate observations of the target person must be taken. Third, a measurement rule relating the two domains must be specified.

The constructive approach to traits gives rise to the traditional or elevation measurement model. A person's score on a trait is that person's sum or average level of behavior within a trait domain. These scores are quite powerful as descriptions of behavior, but are not indices of trait relevance or of the fit between a trait word and an underlying neuropsychic structure.

In the diagnosis of Jane's agoraphobia, consideration of differences between anxious and non-anxious events led to the recognition of an important factor (i.e., that which we label agoraphobia) which largely determined her perception of social situations. Jane's average (or summary) level of anxiety, though certainly important, did not give us this information. Differences among behaviors (*anxious* versus *non-anxious*) and situations (*crowded, unfamiliar places* versus *familiar places with a few friends*) gave rise to finer measurement, and led to an assessment of the fit of agoraphobia to Jane.

Several approaches to the measurement of such differences have been described; all may be characterized as measures of intra-individual *consistency*. In the next chapter, these various approaches are described and compared.

2

Consistency in Personality Measurement

In the last 25 years, there is no issue in personality psychology which has been as hotly debated as that of "consistency". Many would argue that the debate over the consistency of personality has created much heat and little light. It is true that too much effort has been expended investigating unanswerable and unproductive questions (such as "How consistent is personality?"), and too little effort has been expended on more fruitful topics (such as "Where does one find consistency?").

2.1 Actor and observer viewpoints

There is a great deal of confusion in the literature over what is meant by "consistency." Hogan (1986) argues, I think correctly, that much of this confusion stems from the fact that scholars in the field may maintain one of two orientations, seeing personality from the standpoint of the *observer* or from the standpoint of the *actor*. These two perspectives are equivalent to the constructive/biosocial and structural/biophysical perspectives considered in the first chapter.

I cite the actor-observer distinction here because it is particularly useful for understanding the consistency debate. From the actor's perspective, consistency can always be found: My own actions are necessarily consistent, following contingently upon the world as I perceive it. From the standpoint of the observer, consistency is harder to perceive: When I impose my constructs on you, you may appear inconsistently "friendly" or "conscientious." Indeed, actors will only appear consistent to observers when the two share the same ordered set of personal constructs. The constructivists seek to remake the world with observer as criterion; for Norman (1969) the goal would indeed appear to be "To see oursels as ithers see us!" Structuralists seek to understand behavior by standing in the shoes of the actor, as did Lincoln Steffens, the turn-of-the-century muckraker whose analyses of corruption revolutionized American journalism. Steffens - incidentally, a student of Wilhelm Wundt - attained his impact not so much by exposing corruption, but by showing why, from the standpoint of men in power, corruption occurred (Steffens, 1931).

Ultimately, both constructivists and structuralists must bow to empirical findings. In this chapter, I review this literature, consider some different interpretations of "consistency," and begin evaluating the question of whether measures of consistency can contribute unique understanding to the study of personality.

2.2 Empirical studies of consistency: Overview

Studies of individual differences in consistency date back nearly 60 years to the early studies of Allport (Allport & Vernon, 1933), Hunt (1936), and Stagner (1933). In recent years, consistency has been the focus of renewed interest, as investigators have focussed on consistency because of its theoretical implications (Baumeister & Tice, 1988; Bem & Allen, 1974; Chaplin & Locklear, 1988; Lanning, 1988) and/or empirical potential (Chaplin & Goldberg, 1984; Kenrick & Stringfield, 1980; Mischel & Peake, 1982; Paunonen & Jackson, 1985; Tellegen, Kamp, & Watson, 1982; Zuckerman, Koestner, DeBoy, Garcia, Maresca, & Sartoris, 1988).

In spite of a long history of research, the final verdict on consistency has not yet has been reached (cf., Paunonen & Jackson, 1985). The "defense" of consistency has relied primarily (but not exclusively) on the eyewitness testimony of maverick empiricists such as Bem (Bem & Allen, 1974), Kenrick (Kenrick & Braver, 1982; Kenrick & Stringfield, 1980), and others (e.g., Berdie, 1961, 1969a, 1969b; Campus, 1974). The "prosecution" has, in turn, questioned the implications of these studies with the largely (but not entirely) methodological arguments of expert witnesses such as Jackson (Paunonen & Jackson, 1985; Rushton, Jackson, & Paunonen, 1981), Stricker (1966), and Tellegen (Tellegen, Kamp, & Watson, 1982).

My own perspective will be seen to differ somewhat from both of these positions. Much of the empirical literature is indeed flawed, but these flaws are primarily conceptual (i.e., inadequate operationalization of constructs), and only secondarily methodological. Consequently, the arguments advanced by the prosecution on solely technical grounds have been largely misdirected.

Consistency and variability. Investigations into the role of consistency in personality have typically operationalized consistency as the (reversed) amount of intra-individual variability. By intra-individual variability is meant variability over situations or occasions within a domain, rather than variability over trait scores within an individual (see Ozer, 1986). For my purposes, it will be useful to distinguish between two types of intra-individual variability, based on two levels of domain heterogeneity. Global measures of variability are computed across a diverse set of behaviors, that is, within a heterogeneous domain. Specific measures of variability, on the other hand, are computed over a set of behaviors which in principle tap a single trait word, and therefore refer to a relatively homogeneous domain. In both cases, "consistency" refers to invariability or the absence of variability.

2.2.1 Consistency as global invariability

Reliability and convergent validity. In the 1930s, the 1950s, and again in recent years, the global variability of behavior has been a focal topic in personality measurement. In 1933, Allport and Vernon examined relations among a set of 11 measures of intra-individual variability. The measures were heterogeneous both in form and in content, including, for example, measures of variability in errors in estimates of surface area, variability in grip strength, and variability in rhythmic speed. Indices were computed both within and between occasions (Fiske & Rice, 1955). Not surprisingly, the average correlation among these measures was low (.02). But three broader group factors showed strong interrelations (ranging from .28 to .53). This gives weak support to the existence of a generalized variability in the broad perceptual-expressive domain.

Glaser (1952) examined the variability over three separate occasions in three ability measures; taken pair-wise, the number of responses changed from right to wrong (or vice-versa) between any two administrations of any particular test was a good predictor of the number of responses changed between any two administrations for any of the three tests. For example, the correlation between (a) the number of items changed on the mathematics test between the first and second administrations, and (b) the number of items changed on the spatial test between the first and third administrations, was .66. The median of all correlations among variability measures was .67. These results suggest that intra-individual variability scores computed over measures of different abilities will be related.

Campus (1974) asked subjects to generate stories in response to a set of TAT cards. Following this, the subjects were asked to describe the protagonists in their stories using a set of 34 adjectives. These adjectives were combined in pairs to form 17 scales each two items in length. These were treated as self-report measures, and consistency was operationalized as the proportion of variation in responses which was due to the trait scales as opposed to the TAT cards or the interaction/error term. Corrected split half reliability of the measure was .72 for 16 TAT cards. General variability in TAT characterizations, over cards, appears to be a meaningful individual difference construct.

In the self-report domain, Goldberg (1978) administered the MMPI, the California Psychological Inventory (CPI; Gough, 1987), and the Edwards Personal Preference Survey (EPPS; Edwards, 1957) to a sample of 203

University undergraduates. Each test was administered on a separate occasion, and administrations of the same test were separated by four weeks. The number of responses which were changed between administrations, summed over all items in each instrument, provided a general index of consistency. (Goldberg did not report consistencies for individual scales of homogeneous content). In like manner, duplicated items within the CPI and MMPI allowed computation of within-occasion consistencies, and overlapping items between these instruments provided indices of inter-inventory consistency. Corrected odd-even reliabilities for the within-instrument, between-administration consistencies were high, ranging from .69 to .91 (the number of items ranged from 225 to 566). Different measures of consistency correlated fairly well: For example, correlations between variability measures computed from the EPPS and non-overlapping subsets of MMPI and CPI items ranged from .28 to .49. Goldberg concluded that "Indices of response consistency are reasonably homogeneous if they are based upon item pools of considerable size" (p. 287), but that the evidence for a single trait of consistency was "equivocal" (p. 289).

Taken as a whole, these studies of global variability suggest that at least some homogeneity among different measures of variability exists. Globally, some individuals are indeed more variable than others. But what, if anything, does this "g factor" of variability measure?

External correlates. For the present purposes, it will suffice to consider only those studies of general variability within a set of self ratings; I will therefore exclude from consideration investigations into personality correlates of degree of inter-observer consensus (e.g., Petersen, 1965) and studies of the degree of agreement between self and peer (e.g., Tunnell, 1980; Cheek, 1982).

A number of studies have found invariability to be associated with measures of neuroticism. Cattell (1943) found that persons who manifested more variability in their sentiments and attitudes were less elevated on a general factor which he described as *will* or *character*. Block (1961) operationalized Role Variability as the (reversed) magnitude of the first factor in an intra-individual correlation matrix of self-ratings across various stimulus persons. This index was found to be substantially related to a measure of neuroticism derived from the CPI (r = .52). Holden and his colleagues, like Cattell and Block, also found global invariability to be associated with measures of neuroticism (Holden, Helmes, Fekken, & Jackson, 1985).

But the link between inconsistency and neuroticism is equivocated by the report of several studies which reported quite different correlates of consistency. Goldberg (1978) found global invariability to be associated with ego control (on the MMPI) and measures of intellectual interest (on the CPI). A social desirability interpretation has also been proposed (Fiske, 1957). The lack of consensus concerning the empirical implications of global variability may exist because global variability is confounded with stylistic variance, which itself is confounded with measures of many substantive personality traits (Goldberg, 1978; Jackson, 1986). Alternatively, global measures may simply be too heterogeneous to be meaningful, or may be related only indirectly (i.e., as a moderator) to other measures of personality. For these and other reasons, it is worthwhile to consider "specific" or within-trait approaches to intra-individual variability.

2.2.2 Consistency as trait-specific invariability

The trait-specific approach to consistency would appear to have several advantages over the global approach. First, whereas global measures of consistency appear only weakly related to low fidelity, broad bandwidth aspects of personality, trait-specific measures may have more profound and differentiated implications. Second, the global approach is importantly handicapped, for across a broad set of situations, consistency with respect to all trait words is impossible. Only a specific approach can examine ipsative (within-individual, between-trait) differences as well as normative differences in consistency.

Reliability and convergent validity. Berdie (1961) administered ten mathematics subtests of comparable difficulty, each ten items in length, to a sample of University freshmen. The variability in means over the first five subtests was a good predictor of this intra-individual variability over the remaining subtests: Corrected split-half reliabilities for what was, in effect, a 100 item scale ranged from .86 to .91. These reliabilities are impressive, particularly given the fact that the variability measures are in essence deviation scores, taken around the person's mean. Berdie's approach assessed variability within a single occasion. Mitra and Fiske (1956) examined the difference in responding between occasions. These investigators administered seven interest scales and two adjective scales on two occasions, and, for each scale, computed a variability index equal to the number of items changed between administrations. Reliabilities (KR-20) for these derived scores ranged from .34 to .49 for the interest scales, which ranged in length from 14 to 17 items, and from .66 to .70 for the adjective scales, each 56 items in length.

Schneiderman (1980) examined the relations among consistency indices derived from three behavioral measures conceptually related to extraversion in a sample of 34 university undergraduates. The behavioral measures included the amount of eye contact, amount of speaking, and time spent delivering a mock lecture; these were assessed under three situations of varying pull for extraverted behavior. Each measure was standardized (over individuals) within each situation; a consistency score was derived for each measure as the intra-individual variance, over situations, of these standard scores. Correlations among variance measures ranged from .38 to .67; after controlling for relations among simple (mean) scores, residual variance measures intercorrelated from .27 to .42.

Schneiderman also examined relations between his measures of behavioral variability and several paper and pencil measures of variability computed from Bem and Allen's (1974) Cross Situational Behavior Survey (CSBS); this 47-item instrument consists of a set of questions such as "When in a store, how likely are you to strike up a conversation with a sales clerk?", with subjects responses ranging from 1 (not at all) to 7 (extremely). Correlations between Schneiderman's measures and the variability in subject's responses (taken around their own means) to items in the CSBS Friendliness scale ranged from .30 to .59. Correlations between the behavioral measures and a global measure of variability (across CSBS items tapping both Friendliness and Conscientiousness) were lower, ranging from .09 to .40. Schneiderman also computed Bem and Allen's preferred index of consistency, an ipsatized variance measure, equivalent to the ratio of specific Friendliness variance to global CSBS variance. This was modestly related to Schneiderman's other consistency measures, with correlations ranging from .15 to .41.

In sharp contrast to these encouraging results, Chaplin and Goldberg (1984) found little convergence among different measures of consistency. These investigators administered an extended version of the CSBS to 112 subjects, from which ipsatized variance was computed for each of 8 scales. In addition, self-reported consistency, was measured by a single item for each trait (e.g., subjects' response to the question "How much do you vary from one situation to another in how friendly and outgoing you are?"). Subjects also completed a Consistency Questionnaire, which provided a heterogeneous or global measure of consistency for the 112 subjects in their sample. These measures of consistency did not converge. The average correlation, over traits, between the global measure of consistency and the specific ipsatized variance index was -.01. The average correlation between the global measure and self-reported consistency was also - .01. The average correlation between self-reported consistency and the ipsatized variance index, (the two Bem and Allen measures), was only negligibly higher, at .08.

Paunonen and Jackson (1985) also reported negative findings. As with Chaplin and Goldberg, the correlation between ipsatized variance and self-reported consistency was weak (average over 20 PRF scales and ratings was .09). Paunonen and Jackson found that simple intra-individual variance and self reported consistency were, on average, unrelated (a correlation of .02), as were single item self and peer ratings of consistency (.04). Schutz (cited in Paunonen & Jackson, 1985) reported a slightly larger correlation between self and peer ratings of consistency (.27).

These studies of specific variability, when considered as a whole, suggest the following:

(1) In a number of domains, individual differences in consistency, as indexed by within-occasion or between-occasion differences in

responding to paper and pencil inventories, appears substantially reliable.

(2) Different behavioral measures of consistency display substantial coherence, and may also be related to the simple variability in responding to a set of paper and pencil items of homogeneous content.

(3) Self-reported consistency appears unrelated to other measures of consistency, including ipsatized variance, simple variance, and peer ratings.

Although no evidence suggests that single item self-report measures are related to any of the formal measures of intra-individual variability which have been thus far considered, several studies have found that self-reported consistency is related to the degree of convergence among different observer ratings and/or behavioral measures (Bem & Allen, 1974; Kenrick & Stringfield, 1980). If a relation exists between consistency and degree of convergence among so-called criteria, then the average correlation among these criteria will depend upon the level of consistency. In other words, consistency will moderate predictability for that trait (Saunders, 1956).

2.3 Consistency as a moderator variable

The term moderator variable has been used to describe a number of statistical approaches to problems of differential predictability and validity (Zedeck, 1971). I begin by using moderator in the very general sense introduced at the end of the last section, i.e., the dependency of a relation between two variables on the level of a third. Later, a more narrow use of the term will be employed in the discussion of moderated multiple regression.

Logical and psychometric foundation. Consider the consistency of a trait such as dominance. The information which gives rise to the trait of dominance may be thought of as a residing within a universe of items (Cronbach, Gleser, Nanda, & Rajaratnam, 1972; Nunnally, 1978). Items might include, for example, *Dominance with co-worker in task requiring collaboration* and *Dominance in rush-hour automobile driving.*

For the present purposes, the universe of items for dominance-consistency may be taken as the universe of absolute difference scores between all possible pairs of dominance items. (This is, in effect, an intra-individual variance conception of consistency). To the extent that dominance-consistency is a coherent construct, the average intercorrelation among these difference scores within the universe will deviate from zero; that is, dominance-consistency scores based on a random sample from the potential universe of items will be at least nominally reliable.

If consistency is operationalized as the intra-individual variance within a set of items (e.g., on a test), then, to the extent that these items are representative of "items" (including non-test situations) to which one seeks to generalize, then consistency within the set of test items will imply "consistency" or convergence between these items and non-test measures.

With respect to the dominance example, if reliable consistency scores generated from a paper and pencil dominance scale indicate that a person is inconsistent in dominance, then that person should, on average, display a large difference between *co-worker dominance* and *automobile dominance.*

These differences in non-test behavior will lead different observers (the co-worker and the highway patrolman) to different estimates of the person's dominance; these observers will then display less convergence in their ratings than they would for a more consistent individual. On this argument, the effectiveness of consistency as a moderator depends only upon the following:

(1) The representativeness of the sample of items upon which consistency scores are computed,

(2) the reliability of consistency for the particular trait being measured, and, (evidently),

(3) the soundness of the present domain sampling interpretation of measurement (Nunnally, 1978).

Ozer's (1986) conceptualization of consistency as generalizability is, in essence, an extension of this point. Both positions anticipate greater predictability for consistent as opposed to inconsistent persons, and, therefore, a moderator role for consistency in prediction. A moderator effect is also anticipated by the description of individual differences in consistency as differences in reliability (Fiske & Rice, 1955; Goldberg, 1978; Holden et al., 1985): To the extent that persons differ in their reliability, relations with other measures will be differentially attenuated, and persons will differ in their predictability. But in spite of these conceptual arguments, the empirical support for this position is checkered (e.g., Chaplin & Goldberg, 1984; Paunonen & Jackson, 1985).

2.3.1 The Kenrick studies

In Kenrick and Stringfield's (1980) study, a sample of 98 undergraduates provided ratings of elevation, consistency, and observability for 16 traits. For the majority of subjects, peers and parents provided observer ratings of the same three variables for each of the traits. This sample was later supplemented by an additional 76 subjects by Kenrick and Braver (1982).

In the present discussion, I will consider only the combined data presented by Kenrick and Braver (1982); the earlier analyses of Kenrick and Stringfield, apart from being based on a smaller sample, displayed several confounds which rendered their interpretation difficult (Rushton, Jackson, & Paunonen,

1981). The criticism which was directed at the first paper remains important, however, and so will be discussed at some length in the next section.

In the Kenrick and Braver analyses, the average correlation among parent, peer, and self ratings was compared for two groups, namely, that subset of subjects who nominated the trait as their "most consistent", and the entire sample of subjects. This analysis was performed for each of 16 traits. (In Kenrick and Stringfield, "most consistent" and "least consistent" traits were compared. It is unclear why Kenrick and Braver chose to examine unnominated rather than least consistent traits in their reanalysis). The major finding was that the average correlation, over traits, among raters was .47 for the self-nominated "most consistent" trait; in contrast, the average correlation among ratings for unnominated traits was .24. In response to this, Paunonen and Jackson (1985) have argued that the .47 correlation of the most consistent group is likely to be unstable, as it represents an average (across 16 traits) of correlations which are themselves based upon very small sample sizes (the average number of cases per trait was 9).

2.3.2 Consistency and extremity

Rushton, Paunonen, and Jackson (1981) and Block (personal correspondence to Kenrick; cited in Rushton et al.) have suggested that the initial Kenrick and Stringfield results may have been due to a confounding of consistency with trait extremity (see also Glaser, 1952; Mitra & Fiske, 1956; Paunonen & Jackson, 1985). Trait extremity refers to the average absolute distance, over items, between endorsed responses and the scale midpoint. A curvilinear relation between consistency and elevation, and a monotonic relation between consistency and extremity, is to be expected on purely formal grounds. On any measure, a truly extreme score can only be obtained if, over items, consistently extreme values are endorsed. By way of contrast, more central scores can be obtained either by consistent (e.g., rigid selection of the midpoint) or inconsistent response patterns (e.g., alternation between extremes). The particular relation between consistency and elevation will depend upon the extent to which truly extreme scores are represented in the sample; in general, however, one can anticipate an inverted- U relation between variability and elevation. Where the normative mean lies near the scale midpoint, the association between variability and extremity will be monotonic. Consequently, the essence of the expected relationship between variability and extremity can be described by a simple correlation coefficient.

To the extent that measures of elevation and measures of consistency are related, the potential incremental validity of the consistency measure will be constrained. Given the primacy of elevation in contemporary measurement, it is appropriate to describe this as a relationship in which consistency scores are *entailed* by elevation. The extent of entailment of consistency by elevation has been indexed by the correlation between variability and extremity in a number of studies. Paunonen and Jackson (1985) found that the average correlation between intra-individual variability and extremity, over the 20 scales of a Likert scale version of the Personality Research Form (PRF), was .21. Self-ratings appear more susceptible than intra-individual variance measures to the problem of entailment. Rushton et al. (1981) found a correlation of .21 between (self-rated) consistency and extremity. Others have reported somewhat larger coefficients. For example, in the Paunonen and Jackson data, the average correlation between self-rated consistency and extremity was .46. For Stones and Burt (1978), the corresponding figure was .42. Kenrick (correspondence to Block; cited in Rushton et al.) reported an average correlation of .33 in the Kenrick and Stringfield data.

The entailment of consistency scores by elevation scores is problematic for two reasons. The first of these is self-evident, namely, that correlations between elevation and consistency limit the potential informativeness of consistency. The second reason is more subtle: A confounding of variability by elevation may give rise to differences in the distributions of elevation scores between high and low consistent groups. For a bell shaped, bounded set of elevation scores, a positive relation between consistency and extremity will differentially inflate variance in the highly consistent: As the magnitude of this relation increases, the distribution of elevation scores in this group will first flatten, and then approach bimodality. Consequently, the variance of this distribution will increase. It follows that if low-consistent traits are typically rated as moderate in elevation, the distribution of these scores will be restricted, and the variance of these scores will be expected to decrease.

The type of relation one obtains between consistency and normative variance in elevation scores is a function of the particular distribution of elevation scores; as Kenrick and Braver (1982) point out, the relation between extremity and consistency may actually *depress* variability in a high consistent group if the distribution of elevation scores is skewed (i.e., if extreme scores tend to occur at only one end of the distribution).

Because correlations are largely a function of the variances of the measures being related, the expected relationships among elevation measures will be higher for consistent than for inconsistent traits where (a) a positive correlation between consistency and extremity exists and (b) consistency scores sample both tails of the distribution equally. Expected correlations will be greater for inconsistent than for consistent persons where (a) holds but (b) is severely violated. In Rushton et al.'s sample of 52 subjects, elevation scores for 10 of 16 traits showed higher normative variance among subjects who nominated it as "most consistent" than among subjects who nominated it as "least consistent"; the average variance, over traits, was approximately 33% greater for the former group. In Kenrick and Braver's (1982) sample of 174 subjects, seven of the sixteen traits showed higher variance within (a) the sample of subjects nominating it as their "most consistent" trait than within (b) the total sample. The average normative variance in elevation scores for these were virtually identical. Differential variance may not, however, fully account for Kenrick and Stringfield's finding of greater observer agreement in the rating of consistent traits: There was no relation (over traits) between the magnitude of the apparent moderator effect and differential variance in the high *versus* low consistent subgroups (Kenrick & Braver, 1982; cf. Rushton et al., 1981).

Where the effectiveness of a moderator variable is assessed via a comparison of subgroups, these subgroups may differ in variances on measures of interest; further, "criteria" (or, more accurately, target measures) as well as predictor variables (elevation scores) are susceptible to this effect (Chaplin & Goldberg, 1984).

Two remedies may be advanced. The first follows an analysis of McNemar (1969). McNemar found that, although use of subgroups consisting of extreme subjects led to inflated correlation coefficients, errors of estimate remained unaffected. It follows that if one chooses to rely on subgroup analysis, errors of estimate should be examined as well as, if not in lieu of, simple correlation coefficients. Still another remedy is to abandon subgroup analysis altogether. Alternative methods, including moderated multiple regression and Ghiselli's (1960, 1963) differential predictability approach, avoid the problems of conceptual entailment and confounded correlations (Paunonen & Jackson, 1985). The regression approach will be considered in the discussion of the Bem and Allen study which follows.

2.3.3 The Bem and Allen study

Bem and Allen (1974) used subgroup analysis to investigate the extent to which consistency moderates relations among various observer ratings and validity indices in two trait domains, friendliness and conscientiousness, in a sample of 64 University undergraduates. For the trait of friendliness, self-reported consistency was used to split subjects into two groups, high *versus* low consistent. Bem and Allen reported that the average correlation between different measures of friendliness (peer ratings, parental ratings, self ratings, and behavioral indices) was higher for the high consistent group (.57) than for the low consistent group (.27). Individuals low, medium, and high in self rated elevation did not differ in consistency; this suggests that self-rated consistency for the trait of friendliness was unrelated to extremity, but provides only indirect evidence concerning the relative variances of "high" and "low" consistent groups in their elevation on friendliness. The difference between these correlations may, once again, be attributable to different variances in the subgroups being compared (Paunonen & Jackson, 1985).

For the trait of conscientiousness, a somewhat different procedure was used to index consistency. Consistency was operationalized as an ipsatized variance, i.e., the intra-individual variance in responses to the conscientiousness scale over the variation in responses to all CSBS items. Subjects were matched for elevation (mean or sum) on the CSBS conscientiousness scale; individuals were then classified as high or low consistency depending upon whether his or her ipsatized variance score was lesser or greater than that of his or her partner. Consistency so operationalized appeared to be a effective moderator: Persons high on consistency showed greater convergence among ratings and behaviors than did low consistency subjects (.36 *versus* .12, respectively; or .45 *versus* .09 if the *Neatness* measure is excluded from the matrix). Further, because the distributions of elevation scores were matched, this analysis is free of the potential confound of differential variance.

Attempted replications. Chaplin and Goldberg (1984) have weakly replicated Bem and Allen's finding of a moderator effect of consistency for the trait of conscientiousness. These investigators, using the same methods as Bem and Allen, (i.e., ipsatized variance, control for extremity) found average correlations of .27 among criteria for those highly consistent in conscientiousness compared to .16 for those low in this trait.

However, this was the only "successful" moderator effect noted in an analysis of eight traits in which ipsatized variance was used as a moderator; over the eight traits the average predictability for the high and low consistency groups did not differ (.16 *versus* .17). Similar results were found for consistency as determined by self-report and Chaplin and Goldberg's Consistency Questionnaire (in both cases the average correlations were .18 and .16 for the high and low consistency subgroups, respectively).

Paunonen and Jackson (1985) also found that self-rated consistency and ipsatized variance did not reliably enhance predictability: These measures each significantly ($p < .05$) moderated the predictability of only 1 of 20 traits, a finding clearly consistent with chance.

Mischel and Peake (1982) reported a successful moderator effect using ipsatized variance in the prediction of observer ratings of conscientiousness; average correlations among self and peer ratings were .68 for the highly consistent group as opposed to .22 for the low consistency group. They reported a failure to replicate, however, for the prediction of behavioral indices (cf. Funder, 1983). Both results should be viewed with caution, however, as it is unclear from the published report whether these investigators controlled for the potentially confounding effect of extremity.

The cumulative weight of these studies suggests that Bem and Allen were far too sanguine in their assessment of the role of consistency in prediction. However, these replications and failures to replicate are consequential only to the extent that the original study was methodologically and conceptually sound.

2.3.4 Moderated multiple regression analysis

Tellegen, Kamp, and Watson (1982) have argued that, in assessing the contribution of ipsatized variance to the predictability of conscientiousness, Bem and Allen's methods were inadequate. Instead of subgroup analysis (i.e., the comparison of consistent *versus* inconsistent subjects), Bem and Allen should have employed moderated multiple regression to test the hypothesis of differential predictability (Saunders, 1956). In the multiple regression model, the moderator hypothesis is that the correlation between measures (e.g., between *punctuality* and *homework thoroughness*) will vary continuously as a function of consistency scores. consistency will, in other words, interact with homework thoroughness in the prediction of punctuality. The linear X linear component of this interaction can be represented as the product of homework and consistency after main effects have been partialed (Cohen, 1978; Cohen & Cohen, 1975).

In the prediction of punctuality, three independent contributors can be isolated, i.e.,

(1) homework thoroughness (X_1),
(2) ipsatized variance (X_2) with X_1 partialed, and,
(3) an interaction term (X_3), equal to the product of X_1 and X_2 after the main effects of X_1 and X_2 have been partialed.

In a hierarchical analysis, the two main effects are considered prior to the interaction term. The magnitude of the moderator effect can then be estimated by the increment in predictability (indexed by R^2; cf. Ozer, 1985) that follows entry of this final term in the regression analysis.

In examining the predictability of conscientiousness, Bem and Allen used the (ipsatized) variance of the CSBS conscientiousness items as their measure of consistency. Tellegen and his colleagues argue that they should have considered the simple sum of the CSBS conscientiousness items as well as the more complex variance term. The appropriate regression would then include three orthogonalized main effects (homework thoroughness, CSBS conscientiousness [sum], CSBS conscientiousness [variance]), and the three two-way interactions among all pairs of these variables. In the hierarchical analysis described by Tellegen et al., the variance main effect is entered only after the mathematically simpler indices. Similarly, interactions involving the variance term, such as the variance x homework thoroughness interaction of interest, follow entry of the interaction between the simpler scores. Using hypothetical data, Tellegen et al. demonstrate that inclusion of the simple sum of CSBS conscientiousness items leads to greater predictability.[1]

---

[1] In their analysis, Tellegen et al. decompose the variance term into mathematically simpler components, i.e., squares and cross-products of CSBS items. For the present purposes, parsimony would be sacrificed by such an analysis: the interpretation of the contribution of mathematical components such as item sums of squares or cross-

Paunonen and Jackson (1985) have also argued that moderated multiple regression is the appropriate method for testing moderator effects. This method avoids the problem of differential variances encountered by subgroup analyses and statistically controls for potential relations between elevation and consistency. Further, where theory dictates a continuous rather than discrete effect of the potential moderator, as in the present case, multiple regression will be a more powerful technique than the arbitrary dichotomization into subgroups.

In most cases, moderated multiple regression appears fully appropriate for examining the hypothesis of a moderator variable or an interaction. The method is not without controversy, however.

Moderated multiple regression analysis: Controversies. Althauser (1971) and Morris, Sherman, and Mansfield (1986) have noted the prevalence of linear dependencies, or multicollinearity, among linear and simple product terms. Multicollinearity is a problem in hierarchical analysis because, where it exists, estimates of beta weights are not stable (Cohen & Cohen, 1975). Morris et al (1986) argue that significance tests of collinear effects lack statistical power, and that the effect of this multicollinearity has been to severely depress the incidence of significant moderator effects. They recommend supplanting the ordinary least squares regression approach with a principal components regression. This latter method is a regression analysis performed on a reduced set of (substantially non-zero) principal components. Unfortunately, estimates of beta weights produced by this method are biased; further, as Cronbach (1987) has shown, moderator effects which may appear when this approach is used are likely to be illusory.

But this is not to say that the simple regression model discussed by Paunonen and Jackson (1985) is always the method of choice in the testing of hypothesized moderators. Where the hypothesized effect of the moderator is non-linear, the simple product term will not capture the moderator effect, and either subgroup analysis (with more than two groups) or a quadratic regression analysis should be applied. The multiple subgroup approach was examined by Zedeck, Cranny, Vale, and Smith (1971); these investigators found that the GPAs of moderately anxious students were more predictable (from ACT scores) than those of extreme groups; this moderator effect (which was manifested by differential errors of estimate as well as significantly different correlations between groups) was missed by the linear multiple regression approach. Regardless of the approach, it is a misunderstanding of hypothesis testing to infer that, if an interaction term fails to achieve statistical significance, then a moderator effect does not exist (e.g., Cronbach, 1987).

---

products is less straightforward than the interpretation of a theoretically grounded, though mathematically more complex, measure of "consistency."

2.4 Consistency as scalability

The technical concerns cited in the preceding paragraphs compromise the value of the empirical study reported in the Bem and Allen (1974) paper. They should not, however, overshadow the paper's conceptual contribution, which largely accounts for the important impact of the article.

Bem and Allen supplied a convincing rationale for investigating consistency as a moderator variable. But the model described by Bem and Allen in their theoretical discussion was, in fact, considerably more complex than that which they subsequently tested (see also Lay, 1977). Because of this, Bem and Allen's empiricism did not provide an adequate test of their theory.

In the introduction to their paper, they present the idea that what is meant by consistency is *scalability*. For the time being, we can characterize scalability as the degree to which one maintains a normative ordering of situations or items. Bem and Allen describe two individuals; one appears consistent with respect to the trait of friendliness:

> Consider, for example, the 'friendliness' of the second author. She is very friendly to undergraduates in her office, moderately outgoing in a small seminar, and somewhat reserved before a large class ... we do not judge her to be inconsistent any more than we judge a student to be inconsistent when he [she] solves an addition problem but fails a calculus problem (Bem & Allen, 1974, p. 509).

The other individual, by contrast, appears inconsistent:

> ... consider the 'friendliness' of the first author ... He is rather formal with undergraduates who appear in his office, moderately outgoing in a small seminar, and open, personable, and friendly before a sea of 300 faces in introductory psychology ... he appears not 'moderately friendly' but 'blatantly inconsistent'. (p. 509).

In Figure 2.1, the responses of Allen (the "second author" in the above passage) and Bem (the "first author") are described in an ordered two-space of behaviors and situations. The particular scaling of behaviors and situations will be discussed in the next chapter. For the present purposes, it will suffice to note that both profiles are equally *variable* (i.e., show equivalent deviations around their own profile means), but, as Bem and Allen note, they differ in *consistency*. Behavioral variability does not imply inconsistency, nor does a lack of behavioral variability (behavioral rigidity) imply psychological consistency. Rather, a person is consistent in a trait domain if he or she orders situations in a normative fashion. As we are outside of the domain of ability measurement, this parameter of items seems better described by the term *evocativeness* than by the more traditional label of *difficulty*.

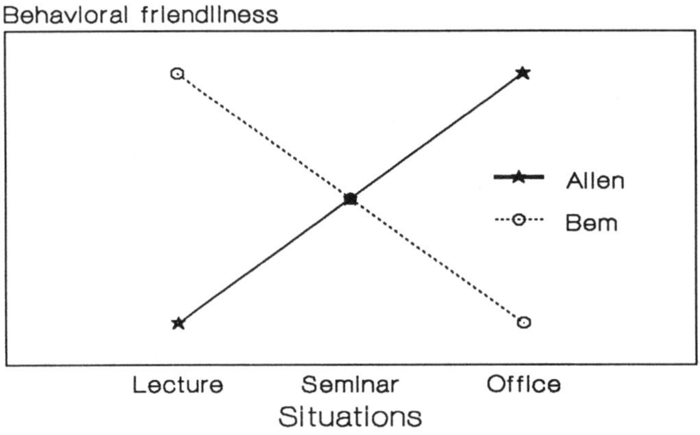

Figure 2.1: Bem and Allen's "Friendliness" (after Bem & Allen, 1974).

Given this definition, Bem and Allen's operationalization of consistency as ipsatized variance appears to be a *non sequitur.* The variance over unstandardized items in a trait domain is simply not equivalent to the scalability definition they defend here. It should be emphasized that, to the extent that this scalability approach is mathematically dissimilar to intra-individual variance (a topic to be addressed in Chapter 3), both the technical and the empirical concerns of Bem and Allen's critics are misdirected.

2.4.1 Two roles for scalability in personality measurement

Two potential functions for measures of consistency in measurement can be considered (Tellegen, Kamp, & Watson, 1982). The first of these is that consistency may moderate predictability, or, equivalently, interact with predictor measures. The second potential role for consistency is as a main effect in prediction. Thus far, I have addressed only the first of these.

With some traits, a direct relation between consistency and criteria seems plausible. One would expect that highly conformist persons, for example, will appear highly consistent (scalable) relative to non-conformists. Similar arguments could be presented for related traits such as ego-control, socialization, and conscientiousness. For these constructs, at least, a theoretical rationale can clearly be derived for hypothesizing a zero-order correlation between scalability and traditional measures. In a multiple regression analysis, consistency may contribute as a main effect as well as a moderator.

2.4.2 Scalability in personality theory

In the previous chapter, I argued that the assessment of the *fit* of a trait word to a person is a central problem for personality psychology. In the present chapter, empirical findings have been described which have examined the role of consistency in largely pragmatic problems of prediction, and scalability has been introduced as a reasonable conceptualization of consistency. In this section I attempt to relate these two rather diverse topics by examining the soundness of scalability as an index of fit. If scalability is an appropriate measure of fit, then a trait word such as friendliness will fit an individual to the extent that the individual responds to situations in terms of their tendency to evoke friendly behavior.

The notion that scalability is a measure of fit may be considered from two perspectives. The first of these is descriptive: Is scalability used as a measure of fit in lay usage? The second perspective is prescriptive or normative: Should scalability be used as a measure of fit in personality assessment?

Descriptive argument. The descriptive argument has been presented by Bem and Allen, who argue that, in lay assessment, we typically choose a set of trait words which "fit", and that fit is indexed by scalability:

> We will describe the second author as moderately friendly rather than inconsistent because we recognize the underlying Guttman scale to which her behavior [in situation] conforms. But when we encounter the first author, whose behavior does not scale according to the recognized 'friendliness' dimension, we will typically try to repartition his behaviors before accepting a verdict of inconsistency. Thus, the first author is, perhaps, a moderately aloof chap who is a great stage performer (p. 510, bracketed clause added).

Scalable behavior leads to the application of the trait word *friendly*, and non-scalable behavior leads to the use of other trait terms, i.e., "aloof ... performer". This characterization of lay usage appears plausible, but, as I will argue in the next chapter, it conflicts with the traditional measurement approach. Popular usage fails, in any event, to provide a satisfactory characterization of fit: "Fit" describes the degree of similarity of intrapsychic structure to normative construct, not the normative probability of describing someone with a particular trait word (see Chapter 1).

Normative or prescriptive argument. The argument for scalability as a measure of fit hinges on four points. The first three have been discussed previously, and are considered non-controversial; the fourth will require further elaboration.

(1) With respect to personality traits, situations differ along many dimensions. For example, situations differ in their tendency to evoke friendly behavior, playful behavior, and achievement- oriented behavior.
(2) People will be differentially sensitive or responsive to different dimensions upon which situations differ.
(3) Across a broad set of situations, consistency (scalability) with respect to all trait words is impossible. Situations may make competing demands upon the individual, or offer competing rewards to the individual (e.g., a party during finals week to a university undergraduate).
(4) If measurement is sufficiently reliable (generalizable), a highly scalable pattern of behavior provides firm evidence for a parallel personality structure.

The first three points reflect the presence of both ipsative and normative variability in the extent to which traits are scalable for persons. The fourth point argues that, if a person behaves in a scalable fashion in a trait domain, then the representation of situations on that dimension (that is, their scaling for evocativeness) captures much of the important variation in those situations for the individual. Such a person would be particularly sensitive to differences on this dimension. This sensitivity suggests the presence of a cognitive schema, or structure, which processes information in a way which corresponds to the normative scaling of the dimension (Markus, Smith, & Moreland, 1985).

Sensitivity, or high scalability, suggests that the trait word is an important one for the individual in perceiving and responding to the world. Because of this, the assessment of scalability provides a subtle approach to the measurement of personal constructs (Kelly, 1963). Over a set of situations in which different perceptual strategies are normatively equally viable, a person's choice of a particular strategy tells us something about the person. If behavior is reliably scalable within a trait domain, the mechanism which generates this perceptual-behavioral sensitivity can only be a personality structure.

Consequently, high scalability indicates the presence of a personality trait or structure. The appropriate label for this structure, however, may or may not be the trait word which describes the particular ordering of situations and behaviors within which scalability is assessed. But even if, for example, high dominance-scalability is not what we ordinarily label as "dominance", it can still tell us something important about the person, and is consequently of interest to personality assessment.

2.5 Summary

In this chapter, prior empirical investigations of the properties of within-individual consistency were examined. First, a global approach to consistency was considered; though some global measures are reliable, this approach lacks differentiation, and is logically hampered by real world constraints. (It is impossible to maintain perfect consistency with respect to traits which are not orthogonal). A specific or within-trait approach to consistency was then examined. Empirical findings suggesting that consistency moderates predictability are of uncertain significance because of failures to replicate, possible methodological shortcomings, and, most importantly, by an improper operationalization of "consistency".

By "consistency" we mean, and should mean, "scalability". A person will be scalable, for a particular trait, to the extent that he or she perceives differences between situations (in their evocativeness for that trait) in a normative fashion. This approach maintains an important advantage over the conception of consistency as simple behavioral rigidity or invariability, in that it recognizes that consistency need not imply invariability. A person can be responsive to changes in the environment and still be consistent with respect to a particular trait word.

For some traits, scalability measures may relate directly to relevant criteria, functioning as main effects in prediction. More generally, scalability should operate as a moderator variable, that is, it should interact with other measures in the prediction of criteria. Because scalability provides an index of fit, and thus can potentially provide additional insight into personality, exploratory analyses examining the properties of scalability measures against known marker variables are also sanctioned.

3

Scalability and Elevation

At the end of the first chapter, two approaches to measurement were introduced, elevation and consistency. In the second chapter, several interpretations of consistency were considered, leading to the conception of consistency as scalability. In the present chapter, the two approaches of elevation and scalability are made more explicit, and some rudimentary statistical properties of the scalability approach are discussed. Scalability is compared with measures of response idiosyncrasy with roots in the cognitive domain, including measures of person fit (Smith, 1986; Wright, 1977) and test appropriateness (Hulin, Drasgow, & Parsons, 1983). Some reasons for assessing scalability are presented.

3.1 Elevation

When persons are asked to characterize a behavior with respect to a trait, as in "How *friendly* is helping a *distressed motorist?*", one of several yardsticks might be used to arrive at a response. Ratings may be based upon an assessment of intensity (what the person risks or sacrifices by the behavior), extremity (the normative likelihood of such a behavior), or some combination of these.

In spite of the availability of several metrics, people display a reasonable amount of consensus when asked to score behaviors on trait dimensions (see, for example, Table 4.1). Consensus emerges, in part, because intensity and extremity are highly confounded: One reason that normatively extreme behaviors are rare is that they are typically costly, in the sense that the individual must forego other opportunities or take substantial risks. Examples of behaviors which are both normatively rare and costly for the individual are readily conceived, including, for example,

Join North Pole expedition (high Adventurousness),
Run for political office (high Dominance), and
Spend many years in graduate school (high Achievement-orientation).

Given the pervasive confounding of intensity and extremity, we may fairly speak of a single metric. When persons are asked to rate behaviors for traits, the average, over persons, of such ratings is what I will refer to as the elevation of the behavior for the trait. That is, the *elevation* of behavior x for trait word k refers to the rated magnitude (extremity or intensity) of behavior x for trait k.

Elevation and prototypicality. This discussion of "elevation" differs, at a conceptual if not empirical level, from the more purely semantic characterization of behavior-trait relationships as varying in *prototypicality*. In the present context, prototypicality refers to the goodness of fit of a behavior within a trait category, or the perceived centrality of the behavior within a trait domain. Though investigators have typically assessed prototypicality by simply averaging over ratings of prototypicality (Buss & Craik, 1980, 1983; Hampson, 1982a), one could argue that the concept of prototypicality might be equally well represented by the standard deviation of ratings of elevation. Prototypicality is attractive because it represents behavior-trait relationships by a single index, but behaviors which differ in prototypicality may differ in their elevation and/or in the degree of consensus about their elevation. (Degree of consensus about ratings of prototypicality, however, may be constant across levels of prototypicality [see Buss & Craik, 1984, Table 1]).

3.1.1 Person scores

Under the elevation model, a person's score for a trait is simply the sum, over items (opportunities, situations), of behavior scores. The model can be represented as follows:

$$\begin{aligned} \text{Elevation}_{ik} &= \Sigma\,(X_{ijk})/N_{\text{situations}} \qquad (1) \\ &= \Sigma\,(X_{i.k}) \end{aligned}$$

The elevation score for person $_i$ on trait word $_k$ is simply the average, over situations, of the elevation scores for behaviors exhibited by that individual. This representation is general, and characterizes both a simple frequency approach (behaviors are scored as simply 0 or 1) and more complex weighting schemes.

3.1.2 Role of the situation

The act frequency approach (Buss & Craik, 1983) is the prototypical modern instantiation of the elevation model. An important feature of the act frequency approach is that, as with all elevation approaches, the relation between behavioral elevation and estimated trait scores does not vary within a broad range of situations.

In an early paper on the act frequency approach, Buss and Craik (1980, p. 383) described the following act as prototypically dominant:

He (she) readily used the authority of his (her) position.

On the elevation model, this act will scored the same for dominance regardless of the situation in which it arises. If this method were used to estimate the dominance of a college instructor, for example, the inference one would make about dominance would be the same if this individual "used authority" in either of the following situations:

An emotionally distressed student comes to office hours seeking compassion (or)

Proctoring an examination

The failure to consider situational context is a limitation of the pure elevation approach, and it cannot be solved by simply providing more detailed descriptions of acts. A relatively contextualized act, such as Buss and Craik's

On the auto trip, he [she] decided which directions to take when they got lost (1980, p. 384)

may still hide a range of situations which vary in their demands for dominance. The "auto trip" may refer, for example, to either a

Sunday drive through the country with spouse (or)

Trying to find the hospital emergency entrance with a wounded child

Again, on the act frequency approach, this act is considered prototypically dominant regardless of the situation in which it arises. Block (1989) has recently discussed this and other limitations of this model. For my purposes, it will suffice to note that the failure to systematically incorporate situational information in trait inference severely hampers the elevation approach to measurement.

3.2 Scalability

As defined in the last chapter, scalability with respect to a particular trait refers to the tendency to behave in a manner concomitant with situational demands. The formalization of scalability rests upon defining appropriate parameters of behavior and situation. The appropriate term to characterize behavior has already been introduced, it is behavioral elevation. The corresponding situational parameter is *evocativeness*: The evocativeness of situation j for trait word k refers to the average elevation of behavior (measured with respect to trait word k) manifested by persons in situation j. "Situation" is used here in an entirely general sense which includes social and cultural as well as physical properties (Argyle, Furnham, & Graham, 1981; Magnusson, 1978).

As *situation* is used to characterize both the focal stimulus and the ambient environment (Cattell, 1983), different items on personality inventories may be said to constitute different situations. Similarly, the endorsement of different paper and pencil responses, though motorically similar, are best understood as different behaviors, in the same sense that

Writing a love letter, *Writing a shopping list*, and *Writing a philosophical treatise* are best understood in terms of their differences rather than their similarities.

If for a particular trait, a subpopulation of persons, situations, and behaviors could be abstracted for which a perfect association was maintained between evocativeness and elevation, several consequences would follow. The rank order of these persons, scored according to the elevation of the behaviors they manifest, would be invariant across these situations. Similarly, the rank order of situations, scored according to the elevation of the behaviors they evoke, would be invariant across persons. In short, the referenced trait word would be perfectly *scalable* (Guttman, 1950; Bem & Allen, 1974). It is for this reason that the approach is described as the scalability model.

In spite of this similarity, several differences between the present scalability approach and that of Guttman (1950) can be noted. First, the raw scores which comprise the matrix within which scalability is to be assessed are, in the present model, multi-valued rather than dichotomous. If the relatively continuous values of a matrix which is perfectly scalable are rendered dichotomous, via the use of any intermediate cutting point, the resulting matrix will then be perfectly Guttman-scalable.

For example, consider a perfectly scalable sample of persons, situations, and behaviors for the trait of sociability. Behaviors manifested by the sample of persons may be scored as to their sociability-elevation. These scores may then be rendered dichotomous by choosing a cutting point; behaviors which are more sociable than, for example, *Saying hello to a remote acquaintance* would be assigned the value of 1, while other behaviors would receive the value of 0. Discounting ties, the properties of rank order invariance of persons over situations and of situations over persons would hold perfectly in such a matrix; Guttman scalability would therefore also be perfect.

Unlike the Guttman approach, the present approach is a metric, rather than non-metric method. A metric approach is employed here because it allows that certain ordinal violations may be trivial, and recognizes that not all ordinal differences are equally important. Concern over scale type is, in any event, largely unwarranted: Nunnally (1978, p. 28) has argued that the assumption of metric properties which one's scale lacks (e.g., assuming interval properties for a scale in which only ordinal statements are technically sound) will, in general, have only a negligible impact on results.

The final, and most important, difference between the present approach and that of Guttman is one of emphasis. Whereas the traditional model examined the degree to which *items* contribute to the scalability of a measure (Guttman, 1950), the present approach is instead concerned with individual differences in the extent to which *persons* contribute to an overall estimate of scalability.

This emphasis on individual differences in scalability is, empirically, somewhat unusual. Though Fiske (1963) drew attention to the difference between simple error variance and "idiosyncrasy", he did not consider treating individual idiosyncrasy as a personality variable. An important exception to the neglect of individual differences in scalability is an early paper by McReynolds (1951), in which the scalability of Rorschach responses among three groups was examined. The groups consisted of 160 psychiatric inpatients, 25 persons of below-normal intelligence, and 54 non-psychiatric controls. Subjects in all samples were asked to detect the presence or absence of fifty images on a series of Rorschach cards. The probability of an affirmative response in the non-psychiatric group was used as a basis for scaling the images. This normative order was then compared with subject's own pattern of responses. Not surprisingly, McReynolds found more and greater deviations from the normative order for the two deviant subjects than for the controls.

The scalability model may be represented as follows:

$$\text{scalability}_{ik} = - \Sigma\, d_{ijk}, \qquad (2)$$

where

$$d_{ijk} = \Sigma\, |X_{ijk} - (X_{.jk} + X_{i.k} - X_{..k})| \qquad (3)$$

That is, trait word *k* fits person *i* to the extent that the sum of the observed deviation scores (d_{ijk}) is small (Equation 2). Each deviation score is equivalent to the absolute value of the difference between the observed score (X_{ijk}) and the expected score. This expected score may, in turn, be broken down into its components: It is the person's elevation, $X_{i.k}$, (the expected score given the person), plus the situation's evocativeness, $X_{.jk}$, (the expected score given the situation), minus the mean over all persons and situations for the trait, $X_{..k}$.

3.2.1 Scalability and the ANOVA approach to consistency

Generally, the information available for judgements about a particular personality trait may be represented as a matrix of persons by situations, with entries representing behavioral elevation. In such a matrix, the person's elevation and the situation's evocativeness may be viewed as main effects, with the remaining variance representing a confounding of interaction and measurement error. This matrix can then be described using variance components (the ANOVA approach) or generalizability coefficients.

In the ANOVA approach, variance components are computed for persons, situations, and the person X situation interaction. Typically, the presence of an additional response mode component unconfounds measurement error from the two-way interactions (e.g., Bishop & Witt, 1970; Dworkin & Kihlstrom, 1977; Endler, Hunt, & Rosenstein, 1962; Endler & Hunt, 1966, 1969; Moos, 1968).

The major focus in the ANOVA approach has been the comparison of different variance components; these comparisons have been used as indices of the relative importance of person, situation, and interaction. But such comparisons are futile. Ozer (1986, p. 29) has described the "impossible necessity" of sampling equally along all facets (e.g., persons, situations) if comparisons of different variance components are to be interpretable. Ozer advocates the use of generalizability coefficients rather than variance components (see also Fiske, 1963). Generalizability coefficients describe the robustness of a particular effect (such as a main effect for persons) over levels of other facets (for example, situations). Golding (1975) has presented similar arguments. Ozer's approach is noteworthy because he argues that different generalizability coefficients describe different types of consistency, such as the consistency of individual differences over situations or of situation effects over persons.

The ANOVA and generalizability approaches to person X situation matrices may be compared to the present scalability approach. Perfect scalability for a sample of persons and situations implies, in ANOVA terms, no interaction. Any effects of persons and situations in such a matrix would be perfectly generalizable. The ANOVA and generalizability approaches have the apparent advantage of disentangling the main effects of both persons and situations. But the advantage is questionable. In the ANOVA approach, these effects are uninterpretable. In the generalizability approach, both coefficients depend upon the same interaction term. It is this term, and not the main effects, which reflects the presence or absence of dispositions in the sample of persons under study (Argyle & Little, 1972). Most importantly, the scalability approach provides a measure of individual differences in the contribution to the interaction term. These individual differences in scalability are neglected by the ANOVA and generalizability approaches.

3.3. Some statistical properties of elevation and scalability

Statistical power. Elevation scores represent aggregates over items, situations, or opportunities. As aggregates, these measures are statistically powerful: The Spearman-Brown formula guarantees that the reliability of a minimally-coherent measure increases with the number of items from the universe of interest (Nunnally, 1978). On the classical model, the simple summation of such items insures that true-score variance will increase relative to error variance. Items may be dispersed in time (Epstein, 1979) or presented on a single occasion, as with inventory scales (e.g., Gough, 1975).

Scalability scores, on the other hand, are essentially deviation scores. These scores are necessarily less stable than the means (i.e., the person's elevation and the situation's evocativeness) around which the scores are computed. This lack of stability implies that scalability measures will be less reliable than the elevation scores around which they are computed (Tellegen, 1988).

Non-monotonicity. At the end of Chapter 2, it was argued that a person may perceive and respond to the world in terms of dominance, i.e., be highly scalable, but not appear high in elevation for the trait of dominance (see also Baumeister & Tice, 1988). The converse of this also holds: A high elevation score for a trait such as dominance need not imply that the person perceives and responds to the world in terms of the normative dimension.

Conceptually, scalability and elevation scores are different. We expect elevation scores to maintain monotonic relations with criteria (e.g., Magnusson & Endler, 1977). By contrast, relations between scalability scores and traditional criteria will, for most persons and situations, not be monotonic. In a given situation and for a given person, as the elevation of behavior increases, the scalability of the behavior will first increase, then decrease. Scalability is maximized at that point at which behavioral elevation and situational evocativeness are, for the assessed person, concordant.

This lack of monotonicity may be illustrated. Consider the following situation encountered by an undergraduate:

You are in a large lecture with a few friends and are bored.

Assume that this situation is empirically determined to be "medium" in its evocativeness of friendliness. For the undergraduate whose elevation score is empirically determined to be low or moderate, the estimate of friendliness that would be made if the person behaves in a highly sociable way, e.g.,

Laugh or do something silly

would be *lower* than if the person were to endorse an empirically more moderate behavior such as

Act responsibly; do the right thing.

Predictions such as this, when viewed from the perspective of the traditional elevation model, may appear counterintuitive. From this analysis, it would appear that main effects of scalability will be at best complexly related to traditional elevation measures.

3.4 Anticipated relations among measures of elevation, scalability, and variability

Elevation and scalability. In the last chapter, the problem of entailment of variability scores by elevation scores was considered. Subsequently, the notion of scalability was introduced. The extent of likely entailment of scalability scores by elevation scores has not yet been considered.

The degree and direction of constraint of scalability scores by elevation scores will depend upon the range of behaviors, situations, and persons sampled. That is, extremely elevated persons in extremely evocative situations may obtain predicted scores which are more extreme than is provided by the response format, where predicted scores are equal to the average of behavior and situation effects, (or elevation + evocativeness - main effects). In this case, an extreme elevation score would entail a moderate to large scalability score. On the other hand, if the set of situations is such that an extreme situation has a much greater variance (i.e., lower pull) than the remainder of situations, then responses to that situation will be a prime determinant of elevation scores, and an extremely elevated person will necessarily endorse an extremely elevated behavior in that situation, thereby obtaining a low to moderate scalability score.

It would appear that the relation between scalability and elevation is not *a priori* specifiable on formal grounds, but depends upon the content of the measure, its response format, and the sample investigated. However, if simple variability is highly entailed by elevation, and variability and scalability are highly related, then entailment of scalability by elevation can be anticipated. Expected relations between scalability and elevation, then, may be seen as largely contingent upon relations between scalability and intra-individual variability.

Scalability and variability. Both scalability and simple intra-individual variability refer to variation around expected values. In the case of scalability, the expected value is derived from the scores of both the person and the situation (i.e., elevation and evocativeness). In the case of simple variability, the expected value is computed from the person's scores alone. If scalability is assessed over a set of situations which are equal in evocativeness, then the evocativeness of each situation will equal the grand mean, and the effect of the situation will wash out (see Equation 2). Scalability and variability will then be equivalent, except in two minor regards. First, variability scores are computed from squared rather than absolute deviations. Second, scalability scores are reversed in direction from simple variability scores. These differences are minor. Essentially, scalability scores and intra-individual consistency scores will be equivalent to the extent that the items or situations are similar in evocativeness.

If intra-individual variability is computed on a set of situations which have been previously standardized, the variability scores will differ from scalability computed on raw scores in only three regards, i.e., the two noted above and, in addition, the effect on scalability scores of differential item variances, which are partialed out by standardization.

In light of this discussion, two of the studies of variability discussed in the previous chapter pertain quite directly to the measurement of scalability. Berdie (1961) reported that the cognitive subtests over which he assessed consistency were equal in difficulty; he found variability scores to be reliable and to function weakly as moderators. Schneiderman (1980) computed variability on a set of standardized situations; he reported substantial correlations among different behavioral indices of consistency. Most studies of variability, including that of Bem and Allen (1974), did not report or control for differential situational evocativeness.

3.5 Scalability and response idiosyncrasy

An idiosyncratic response pattern occurs when the array of responses by a subject appears contrary to that of the group. In the testing of aptitude and achievement, this would be epitomized by the subject who "fails" easy or popular items and "passes" difficult or unusual ones.

There are a number of reasons why such a pattern might appear. One such reason is dishonesty. Consider the struggling student, burdened by low ability. The student muddles through the easiest items and struggles somewhat on those of only moderate difficulty. The more difficult items are taxing, and the student no more than recognizes the material; still, in spite of the subjective difficulty of these items, the student will make marginally educated guesses. With the most difficult items, it is a different story. The student is overwhelmed and clueless; the questions might as well be in a different language.

Confronted with this situation, the student might manifest one of a number of responses. The student might simply guess. Alternatively, the student might become discouraged and self-punishing, or resentful and angry. If the student is sufficiently "resourceful," he or she will look at the paper of a high-ability classmate and attempt to copy answers to the difficult items. A careful inspection of the answers would reveal the tell-tale pattern of response idiosyncrasy, in which easy items are failed and difficult ones are passed. Without such checking, the student would be given a score that he did not earn, one that is *spuriously high* (Hulin, Drasgow & Parsons, 1983).

There are several other circumstances in which an idiosyncratic pattern of responses might occur. For example, a student of moderate to high ability may incorrectly fill out a multiple-choice answer sheet. In particular, the first n responses may be entered correctly, but the student might miss a row of bubbles or enter two responses in the same row. In either event, responses to questions $n+1$ through k will be scored as correct only at the level of chance, due to the carelessness of the respondent, and she would attain a score that is *spuriously low*. An idiosyncratic response pattern might also reveal a pattern of unusual training or even tampering with answer sheets (Hulin et al., 1983).

In the measurement of aptitude and achievement, the problem of response idiosyncrasy has attracted a number of investigators. Approaches to the measurement of response idiosyncrasy include (1) *personal biserial correlations* between the vector of a person's responses and that of a group norm (Chaplin & Locklear, 1988; Donlon & Fischer, 1968), (2) *caution indices* based on the covariance between responses and a Guttman vector of dichotomized item difficulty (Sato, 1975; see Tatsuoka, 1984), (3) measures of *person fit*, marking the extent of deviations of a response vector from a one parameter item response theory (IRT) model (Smith, 1986; Wright, 1977), and (4) *appropriateness indices* based on deviations from a three parameter IRT model (Hulin et al., 1983; Levine & Drasgow, 1983).

These approaches to response idiosyncrasy can be compared with the scalability approach. All of these measures share two features with each other and with the scalability approach. First, each model extracts information from a subject's array of responses beyond the typical summary index. Second, this additional information can be used to characterize the relevance of the summary score for the individual.

Beyond these similarities, some differences among the methods can be noted. The cognitive-based approaches are designed to detect what Tellegen (1988) has called *response aberrance*, that is, the unusual protocol with scores that are held to be uninterpretable under the investigator's measurement model. By contrast, the scalability approach (and related applications of consistency measurement in personality research) are designed to detect far more frequent "violations," indeed, violations which are likely to be sufficiently frequent to render latent trait models inappropriate. A second difference between the scalability model and the alternative approaches is that the latter are designed to work only with dichotomous data (but see Drasgow, Levine, & Williams, 1985). Clearly, a systematic comparison of the various approaches to measuring response idiosyncrasy is called for, particularly one in which the data employed are real (as opposed to simulated), polychotomous (as opposed to true/false), and sampled from the domain of personality (rather than that of ability).

3.6 Why measure scalability?

Three reasons may be specified for measuring scalability. First, scalability provides an index of fit between trait words and structures. Because of this, even if the scalability of a trait word such as irritability does not predict whether or not someone is or should be called "dominant", a phrase such as

Louise sees the world in terms of dominance

remains informative.

Second, scalability provides a theoretically satisfying conception of consistency. Given all of the attention paid to the Bem and Allen study and the simplicity of the method, it is surprising that no investigations of the scalability of conscientiousness and friendliness have appeared in the literature. Individual differences in scalability are essentially untested.

The third reason is more pragmatic. Scalability and elevation can be computed on the same data sets. Any matrix of persons X situations, with quantified or quantifiable entries, can be expressed as a set of marginals and residuals from which scalability scores can then be computed (e.g., Tukey, 1977). Scalability scores can be computed, in other words, on traditional checklists and inventories (see Chapter 7). The possible benefit of the approach is substantial. As scalability and elevation are not perfectly correlated, scalability can contribute information not present in traditional elevation scores. As the cost of computer analysis approaches zero while the value of subjects' time remains high, the promise of this psychologically sanctioned, mathematically simple approach is further enhanced.

In the next four chapters, three empirical studies of scalability will be described.

4

A Single Trait Measure of Scalability

A person's scalability for a trait is a measure of the consistency of that person's behavior over situations. For any trait, sufficient data for measuring scalability include (1) observations of behavior-in-situation, and, (2) a prior metric for assigning elevation scores to the observed behaviors. The generalizability of scalability scores will be enhanced to the degree that the range of situations is representative of the domain of interest. A paper-and-pencil set of "situations" may be considered as a sample from that domain, albeit one which, because of its homogeneity, is lacking in both statistical power and conceptual generality.

4.1 Overview

In the first study to be reported, a brief measure was constructed to assess scalability, variability and elevation for the trait of hostility in a sample of University of California undergraduates. This Situational Hostility Scale (SHS) includes 14 detailed vignettes which describe social situations. These situations are diverse in content, though all depict breaches of territory and/or the frustration of various social or task related goals. A sample item from the scale follows:

> Looking forward to getting a paper back from your TA (although your initial excitement has wavered somewhat ... its been two weeks since you handed it in), you head for what otherwise promises to be a typically boring discussion section. Only this one turns out to be even worse than most. Two hours of repetition of lecture material that was itself redundant. What a waste of time ... you should have stayed in the library and studied for exams. Relieved as you see the TA passing out the papers, but puzzled as you realize that the TA keeps looking away from you. The nervousness and bad hunches suddenly make sense - the last of the papers has been handed out and you're still empty-handed ... a sinking feeling in your stomach as you see that your best paper ever is gone forever, and your TA lost it.

The nine behaviors, or response options, represent rational-empirical clusters derived from a set of 36 simpler elements. These nine response options describe verbal, physical and somatic reactions; they include both actions directed towards an aggressor and more diffuse responses.

4.2 Pretest: Scaling of behaviors

Elevation ratings for the nine response options of the SHS were obtained from a sample of 17 male and 38 female undergraduates enrolled in psychology courses on the Berkeley campus of the University of California; subjects participation in this brief task was on a volunteer basis. In response to the question "*How hostile is this action/feeling?*", subjects provided Likert ratings of the behaviors on a scale which ranged from 1 ("*Not at all hostile*") to 7 ("*Extremely hostile*"). Males rated two behaviors significantly higher than did females, namely, "Shouting orders in anger" and "Agreeing, giving it up, letting it pass". In spite of these differences, the within-sex values were judged sufficiently similar to be combined; these values were then themselves averaged to provide an estimate of behavioral elevation for each of the nine items. The results are summarized in Table 4.1.

TABLE 4.1: PRETEST RATINGS OF NINE BEHAVIORS FOR "HOSTILITY"

Weighted Mean[a]	Behavior	Males Mean S.D.	Females Mean S.D.
6.20	Hitting, kicking, pushing	6.24 0.90 a	6.16 0.97 a
5.47	Leaving and kicking something, slamming the door	5.56 1.18 ab	5.34 1.19 b
5.39	Shouting orders in anger	5.82 1.02 a	4.95 1.04 b*
4.88	Saying something insulting, snapping	5.00 0.79 bc	4.76 1.44 c
4.24	Being sarcastic, saying something to get even	4.24 1.03 d	4.24 1.34 d
4.15	Cursing, swearing	4.41 1.18 cd	3.90 1.27 d
3.91	Gritting your teeth, feeling your face flush	4.12 1.83 cd	3.71 1.47 d
2.86	Frowning, closing your eyes in disbelief	3.00 0.87 e	2.71 1.37 e
1.94	Agreeing, giving up, letting it pass	2.41 1.42 e	1.47 0.89 f*

Note: *N*s = 17 Males, 38 Females. Ratings were made on a 7-point scale with anchors of 1 ('Not at all hostile') and 7 ('Extremely hostile'). Within each column, means sharing a common subscript are not significantly different at $p < .05$.

[a]Weighted mean = (Male average + Female average)/ 2.

*Average ratings of the two sexes differs at $p < .05$.

4.3 Main study

4.3.1 Subjects and procedures

39 University of California sophomores participated in day-long assessments at the Institute of Personality Assessment and Research (IPAR). Subjects were observed by trained assessors in a number of interviews and social settings. Though subjects were paid a nominal sum for their efforts, the non-financial rewards of participation were also presumed salient. These rewards include the prospect of a gain in self-insight, subjective membership in the campus scientific community through participation in research, greater knowledge of personality assessment, and the simple opportunity to self-disclose in a University sanctioned, non-threatening environment.

These subjects were rated by observers using a number of measures. Among these were the California Q-set (CQ-set; Block, 1962) and the Adjective Check List (ACL; Gough & Heilbrun, 1983). Five judges rated each subject using the CQ-set; these judges were joined by five additional observers for the ACL ratings. Prior to the group sessions and interviews, subjects completed a number of paper and pencil questionnaires, including the SHS. One additional subject completed the paper and pencil materials but failed to appear for the group sessions.

Subjects responded to each of the 14 situations of the SHS under two sets of instructions: *What would you feel like doing in this situation*? and *What would you actually do in this situation?*. For each of the 28 items, subjects were asked to provide first, second, and third choices; subjects were informed that these choices did not have to be mutually exclusive.

4.3.2 SHS Scoring

For each item, the three choices were combined into a single weighted index, computed as (3 X first choice) + (2 X second choice) + (third choice). Normatively, these weighted scores were typically similar in mean but smaller in range than first choices alone (this held for 23 of the 28 items; $p < .001$, sign test). The lost variance is assumed to be primarily error variance; the composited responses are, in principle, more robust than the single first choices.

The weighted scores were treated as measures of behavioral elevation for two 14-item scales, which can be abbreviated as *Feeling* and *Action*. Two elevation scores for each person were computed by summing over the items in each scale (see Equation 1, Chapter 3). Scalability scores were similarly computed (Equations 2 and 3). Simple intra-individual variability scores were computed around elevation scores; these measures allow both comparison with earlier studies and an examination of the relation between scalability and variability. Finally, smoothed scalability and variability measures were computed, in which responses were aggregated over sets of 4 to 5 situations of similar evocativeness prior to the determination of deviation scores. These smoothed measures have the same advantages and disadvantages that any smoothed curve has over a more detailed representation of data. The advantage is that major trends should, in principle, become more evident. The disadvantage is that, by smoothing, valuable information may be lost (Tukey, 1977).

4.3.3 Results

Several sets of analyses will be described. Internal analyses of the SHS include the interrelations among the various scales and estimates of the reliabilities of these measures. External correlates of these person measures will then be examined. Finally, item statistics will be considered; these item statistics reflect different psychological properties of the 14 social situations.

Before considering the relations among SHS scales, a comment on the interpretation of these correlation coefficients is in order. On the classical model, the correlation between any two variables is a function of both the relation between true scores on the underlying variables and relations involving error scores on the underlying variables. For independently measured variables, correlations involving error scores will, on average, be zero. For such measures, it is appropriate to estimate the magnitude of the underlying relation between true scores by taking into account the presence of this error, i.e., disattenuating the observed correlation coefficient for the effect of unreliability in one or both measures. In the present study, however, elevation and consistency are not independently measured: All measures within a particular response mode (i.e., Feeling *versus* Action) are derived from the same data set, and rely on the person's mean (or elevation score). Because of this, correlations between observed scores will reflect the presence of shared error variance as well as shared true-score variance. Disattenuation of these correlations, either implicit or explicit, is inappropriate; the best estimate of true relationship may be taken as the correlation between observed scores.

Relations between elevation and measures of consistency. Tellegen, Kamp, and Watson (1982) and Paunonen and Jackson (1985) have argued that measures of consistency can only be useful if they provide information not present in simpler elevation scores. Consequently, the first analysis to consider examines the degree of entailment of consistency scores by elevation scores.

TABLE 4.2: CORRELATIONS BETWEEN CONSISTENCY MEASURES AND ELEVATION

Measure of consistency	Linear correlation r	r^2	Quadratic increment R	R^2	sign	Linear + quadratic R	R^2
			Raw data				
Scalability							
Feeling items	.26	.07	.01	.00	-	.27	.07
Action items	.17	.03	.01	.00	-	.18	.03
Variability (Reversed)							
Feeling items	.38*	.15	.00	.00	-	.38*	.15
Action items	-.10	.01	.00	.00	-	.10	.01
			Smoothed data				
Scalability							
Feeling items	.12	.01	.01	.01	+	.13	.02
Action items	.34*	.12	.00	.00	-	.34*	.12
Variability (Reversed)							
Feeling items	.50*	.25	.01	.01	-	.51*	.26
Action items	-.04	.00	.15	.03	-	.19	.03

Note: N = 39. Feeling = "What I would feel like doing." Action = "What I would actually do."
*$p < .05$

In the present sample, scalability measures showed modest positive relations with measures of elevation. Measures of variability for the simple and smoothed *Feeling* scales showed somewhat stronger relations, although the *Action* measures did not show this trend. The relevant correlations are shown in the first column of Table 4.2.

Simple correlation coefficients may not provide a fair test of the entailment hypothesis: Given the curvilinear relation between elevation and intra-individual variability discussed in Chapter 2, and the similarity of scalability to variability discussed in Chapter 3, tests for a curvilinear relation between elevation and scalability should be undertaken. Paunonen and Jackson advocated two methods for testing the degree of curvilinearity.

The simpler of the two indices of curvilinearity is simply the correlation between the consistency measure and extremity, (here measured by the absolute value of the standardized elevation score). On the arguments of Paunonen and Jackson, a negative correlation is expected between extremity and consistency; that is, more variable subjects should have less extreme means. In the present data, correlations between extremity and corresponding scalability scores ranged from -.12 to .05. Relations between extremity and intra-individual variance measures were somewhat stronger, but were consistently in the direction opposite to the predicted direction; these correlations ranged from .05 to .28.

A more rigorous test of curvilinearity uses polynomial multiple regression. With the consistency measure (i.e., scalability or variability) as the dependent variable, simple elevation is entered in a hierarchical multiple regression analysis followed by the square of elevation. This analysis leads to both an index of curvilinearity (estimated by the increment in R^2 when the squared term is entered) and an index of overall entailment (estimated by the magnitude of the R^2 after both terms are entered). In the present data, the quadratic contribution to R^2 was less than .01 for seven of the eight variability measures. For the eighth (smoothed *Action* variance), an increment of .03 was obtained; however, as with the extremity correlation, this regression coefficient was not in the expected direction.

In summary, the regressions linking SHS measures of elevation and consistency are largely linear. Further, the overall magnitude of entailment is moderate, as indicated by the last two columns of Table 4.2. These results would appear to contradict those of Paunonen and Jackson, who, in their own words, "demonstrated strong empirical relations between measures of trait consistency and measures of trait level [elevation]" (Paunonen & Jackson, 1985, p. 497).

The discrepancy between the present findings and those of Paunonen and Jackson is more apparent than real. Although those authors did find strong relations between elevation and both self-reported consistency and ipsatized variance (mean multiple *R*s of .46 and .51), the entailment of non-ipsatized variance was much less severe (mean multiple *R* of .24). This last figure is comparable to the entailment of variance scores found in the present sample (mean multiple *R* of .30). Indeed, the present data replicate the Paunonen and Jackson finding of a modest relation between elevation and non-ipsatized variance. In the present data, scalability was, on average, less correlated with or entailed by elevation than was variability, with a mean multiple *R* of .23. These relations are not sufficiently strong to preclude the possibility that measures of consistency can contribute information not present in elevation scores.

Relations among measures of consistency. The correlation between the two mathematically independent measures of simple scalability (*Feeling* and *Action*) was .46; this appears low, but is in fact nearly as high as one would anticipate from their reliability estimates (disattenuated r = .93). Associations between simple and smoothed scalability were weaker, suggesting that the smoothed measures fail to capture the meaningful idiosyncratic variation which is measured by simple scalability.

TABLE 4.3 - SHS SCALES: RELIABILITIES AND LINEAR CORRELATIONS

Scale	Elevation		Consistency							
(Length)			Scalability				Variance			
			Raw		Smoothed		Raw		Smoothed	
	1	2	3	4	5	6	7	8	9	0
Elevation										
1 Feeling (14)	*.77*	.35	.26	.17	.12	.01	.38	.00	.50	-.02
2 Action (14)		*.86*	-.03	.17	.11	.34	.04	-.10	.04	-.04
Scalability (raw data)										
3 Feeling (14)			*.49*	.46	.56	-.00	.77	.33	.58	-.28
4 Action (14)				*.50*	.17	.33	.36	.74	.16	-.23
Scalability (smoothed data)										
5 Feeling (3)					*.72*	.09	.49	.07	.51	-.18
6 Action (3)						*.61*	-.00	.32	-.01	.39
Variance (reversed, raw data)										
7 Feeling (14)							*.24*	.41	.84	-.08
8 Action (14)								*.32*	.28	.28
Variance (reversed, smoothed data)										
9 Feeling (3)									*.72*	.16
0 Action (3)										*.49*

Note: N = 39 (correlations), 40 (reliabilities). Reliabilities are best lower bound estimates and are italicized. Feeling = "What I would feel like doing." Action = "What I would actually do."

$^{*}p < .05$

Measures of scalability and variability derived from the same data were reasonably similar: Correlations between comparable measures ranged from .39 to .77. These correlations reflect the formal similarities in the two methods, but are not so high as to imply that simple intra-individual variance performs as a substitute measure of scalability. Again, the relations between these mathematically related measures (unlike that between independent *Feeling* and *Action* measures) reflect the presence of shared error as well as true-score variance. The correlations are shown in Table 4.3.

Reliabilities. Reliabilities of the elevation measures were high. Reliabilities of the simple scalability measures were somewhat lower, but were adequate for scales of this length. The measures of simple intra-individual variance were still more modest. As can be seen by examining the main diagonal of Table 4.3, the smoothed measures of scalability and variability were more reliable than the simple measures.

External analyses. Two marker variables were used as criteria against which the SHS measures could be examined. From the ACL, the number of judges checking the adjective *Hostile* provided one index. From the CQ sort, the average placements (over judges) of items 38 and 94 were summed (i.e., *Has hostility towards others*, and *Expresses hostile feelings directly*).

In a moderated multiple regression analysis, initial correlations between elevation measures and these dependent variables were modest. The increase in predictability following entry of the scalability measures (as an orthogonalized main effect) was trivial, with increments in R^2 ranging from .00 to .02. Increases in predictability were modest following entry of the product term (increments ranged from .00 to .05). Six of these eight product terms (p = .14, sign test) were in the direction predicted by a moderator interpretation of scalability, with more scalable individuals showing a stronger relation between elevation and dependent variables. None of the simple or multiple correlations was statistically significant. Evidently, these modest results (summarized in Table 4.4), should be viewed as tentative, particularly given the small sample size and the documented lack of robustness of moderator effects (Ghiselli, 1963).

TABLE 4.4: SHS MEASURES IN THE PREDICTION OF "HOSTILITY"

	Predictability following						
Target Predictor	Step 1 Elevation		Step 2 Scalability		Step 3 Product		
	R	R^2	R	R^2	R	R^2	Sign
ACL Hostility							
Raw data							
Feeling	.14	.02	.18	.03	.26	.07	+
Action	.10	.01	.16	.02	.17	.03	-
Smoothed data							
Feeling	.14	.02	.14	.02	.27	.07	+
Action	.10	.01	.12	.01	.14	.02	-
CQ Hostility							
Raw data							
Feeling	.29	.08	.29	.08	.29	.09	+
Action	.27	.07	.28	.08	.29	.08	+
Smoothed data							
Feeling	.29	.08	.29	.08	.30	.09	+
Action	.27	.07	.31	.09	.33	.11	+
Averages							
Raw	.20	.04	.23	.05	.25	.06	
Smoothed	.20	.04	.22	.05	.26	.07	

N = 39.

The simple measures of scalability displayed a coherent set of relations with observer ratings. The smoothed measures, though somewhat more reliable than the simple measures, were essentially unrelated to non-test indices. Significant ACL and CQ-set correlates of the simple scalability measures are shown in Table 4.5.

Significant correlates of the Feeling scale include items denoting passivity (e.g., ACL *Unambitious* and CQ *Gives up in the face of adversity*), restriction of impulse (e.g., negative correlation with ACL *Uninhibited*), and a lack of social skills or interests (i.e., negative ACL *Talkative* and *Sophisticated*, negative CQ *Verbally fluent*). Significant correlates of the Action scale also included items denoting restriction of impulse and over-sensitivity to normative expectations (e.g., CQ *Compares self to others. Is alert to real or fancied differences between self and other people.*).

The overcontrol (Block & Block, 1980) of the high scorer could have been anticipated. Arithmetically, the highly scalable subject responded to the items of the SHS in a fashion which paralleled normative expectations. Psychologically, when confronted by real-life as well as paper and pencil situations, the same individual appears unable or unwilling to respond to social demands without considering their normative significance.

Situations. In addition to providing scores for persons, the SHS, (like all behavior X situation procedures), provides several psychologically significant measures of situations (see, e.g., Moos, 1968). Evocativeness (the mean, over persons, of elevation scores in a situation) provides one such index. *Pull*, operationalized as the standard deviation of elevation scores, provides a second index. Pull is similar to the notion of constraint advanced by Price and Bouffard (1974), however, whereas constraint refers to the general restrictiveness of a situation, pull refers to its specific restrictiveness, i.e., the dispersion of behaviors observed on a dimension with respect to a particular trait. The physical setting *undergraduate library*, for example, might give rise to the behaviors *study alone* and *study with others*. These behaviors may be presumed to be close together on the trait of achievement, and relatively separated on the trait of sociability. Hence, the library would have greater pull for achievement than for sociability.

The evocativeness scores for the 14 items cross-validated well across both sex and response mode (average r_{rho} = .87). The situations which were most and least evocative of hostility are shown in Table 4.6.

The pull variable fared more poorly. The rank order of pull (standard deviations) scores of the items was not robust across sex or response mode (average r_{rho} = .14). Pull scores (for situations) appear to be susceptible to the same problem encountered by scalability scores (for situations), namely, these scores are inherently less stable than the means (evocativeness, elevation) around which they are computed.

TABLE 4.5: CORRELATES OF SHS SCALABILITY MEASURES

ACL (10 observers)		CQ Set (5 observers)
Feeling scalability		
.36 Unambitious	.32 Awkward	.45 Gives up in the face of adversity
.33 Quiet		.38 Feels a lack of meaning in life
-.47 Forceful	-.35 Noisy	-.46 Rapid personal tempo
-.42 Assertive	-.34 Ambitious	-.40 Behaves in an assertive fashion
-.42 Dominant	-.34 Enterprising	-.39 Talkative
-.41 Loud	-.34 Headstrong	-.33 Values autonomy
-.41 Opportunistic	-.34 Wise	-.32 Verbally fluent
-.41 Confident	-.33 Aggressive	
-.39 Self-Confident	-.33 Opinionated	
-.38 Individualistic	-.33 Sophisticated	
-.36 Uninhibited	-.32 Nagging	
-.35 Boastful		
Action scalability		
.33 Reserved	.32 Organized	.43 Aware of impression made on others
.33 Self-Controlled		.41 Compares self to others
		.39 Thin-skinned, sensitive
		.37 Judges in conventional terms
-.57 Original	-.37 Changeable	-.53 Self-dramatizing; histrionic
-.57 Zany	-.37 Forgetful	-.48 Engages in fantasy and daydreams
-.50 Hasty	-.37 Individualistic	-.46 An interesting, arresting person
-.50 Humorous	-.37 Noisy	
-.50 Wise	-.37 Restless	
-.48 Impulsive	-.36 Spunky	
-.46 Jolly	-.35 Unconventional	
-.46 Robust	-.35 Frivolous	
-.46 Spontaneous	-.35 Outspoken	
-.45 Generous	-.35 Tough	
-.44 Hurried	-.34 Boastful	
-.43 Courageous	-.33 Careless	
-.42 Excitable	-.33 Irresponsible	
-.42 Mischievous	-.33 Outgoing	
-.41 Reckless	-.32 Blustery	
-.40 Loud	-.32 Forceful	
-.40 Uninhibited	-.32 Pleasure-seeking	
-.37 Adventurous		

$N = 39$. All correlations significant at $p < .05$.

TABLE 4.6: SITUATIONS MOST AND LEAST EVOCATIVE OF HOSTILITY[a]

Most evocative of hostile behavior
Finals week: Your roommate comes home with friends and is loud. (Item 3)
Bicycling: you are run off of the road. (7)
You are driving an ungrateful acquaintance home. (11)
An acquaintance scratches your record at a party. (2)
Least evocative of hostile behavior
Your roommate glares at you. (4)
A drunk sits next to you on the bus. (8)
Your TA loses your best paper. (12)
A panhandler threatens you. (6)

[a]Items are presented in abbreviated form.

Pull scores are also subject to entailment by elevation scores. In the extreme case (a dichotomous item), the variance is completely determined by the item's difficulty level. In the present data, the vectors of average evocativeness and average pull (over sex and response mode) maintained a rank order correlation of -.59, that is, the situations which were most evocative of hostility also showed the largest normative variance. No curvilinear trend was observed: The correlation of pull with item extremity, computed on the sets of ranks, was -.12.

4.4 Discussion

The major findings in the present study include the following:

1) Measures of consistency were only mildly entailed by simple elevation measures.

2) Scalability measures were more reliable than corresponding variance measures, with which they were strongly related.

3) The smoothed measures of consistency were not related to either the simple measures of consistency nor to various observer measures.

4) Two mathematically independent measures of scalability (i.e., *Feeling* and *Action*) were related to observer ratings in the domains of conventionality and impulse control.

The first three points provide empirical support for the contention, put forward in the last two chapters, that scalability is an appropriate, if not superior measure of consistency. The fourth point warrants further discussion.

The observer correlates of scalability indicate that it functioned as a general rather than specific measure of consistency. That is, the correlations reflected the formal property of norm-adherence rather than a more content-laden tendency to perceive situations in terms of hostility, rather than along other, normatively equally viable dimensions.

This may be, in part, because no other dimensions were in fact "normatively equally viable". That is, in a single-trait instrument such as the SHS, the normative significance of each item was relatively unambiguous: As all behaviors and situations were chosen from the single domain of hostility, evocativeness could refer only to hostility-evocativeness. High scorers were more likely to display sensitivity to an implicit (and unintended) demand characteristic to match this normative hierarchy.

In real-world social situations, behavior is simultaneously evaluated on a number of dimensions. When we observe social ebullience, we may make inferences on a diverse set of dimensions ranging from the cognitive (intelligence), and the social (manipulativeness, social ascendance, social status, and extraversion), to the physiological (moderate alcohol consumption). Analogously, on a paper and pencil situation X behavior inventory, behaviors may be simultaneously scaled on a number of traits. In such an instrument, the evocativeness of situations and the elevation of behaviors will be different for different traits. Where subjects may adhere to a variety of norms, the adherence to a particular normative ordering must reflect the content of that dimension as well as the more global property of norm-adherence. Consequently, conventionality should be less important in determining scalability scores for a multivariate instrument than for a single-trait measure.

The multivariate approach has several additional advantages over single trait measures of scalability. First, only a multi-trait instrument can properly examine intrapersonal differences in trait scalability and presumed salience. Second, from the standpoint of respondents, only a multi-trait instrument can provide a range of behaviors broad enough to encompass individual differences in what they would do in any situations of diagnostic significance. Third, only a multi-trait instrument allows examination of the hypothesis that different models (e.g., scalability and elevation) may contribute differentially for different trait words.

In the next two studies, the search for specific scalability continues. In the first of these, a multi-trait behavior by situation inventory is constructed in which multiple scalability measures are derived from the same set of responses. In the second, scalability measures are computed on independent sets of responses from items on the scales of a traditional personality inventory.

5

Development of the Situation Behavior Inventory

The Situation Behavior Inventory (SBI) is a paper-and-pencil research instrument designed to simultaneously assess scalability and elevation scores on a number of traits in a University undergraduate population. In the present chapter, the development of the SBI is described.

In its present form, the measure consists of 102 items (situations). For each item, subjects are asked to choose the behavior, from a set of 18, which most closely corresponds with what they would in fact do if they found themselves in the "real life" equivalent of this paper-and-pencil situation.

The set of items in the SBI, unlike those of the Situational Hostility Scale (SHS) described in the last chapter, are reasonably concise; an effort was made to present a diverse set of items to subjects in a finite period of time. The inventory is included as Appendix 1.

5.1 Sampling considerations

The SBI, and scores to be gathered using the instrument, may usefully be understood to be dependent upon samples from populations of persons, situations, trait words, and behaviors (Cronbach, Gleser, Nanda, & Rajaratnam, 1972; Ozer, 1986).

5.1.1 The sample of persons

The decision to examine scalability in a population of University undergraduates, rather than in an alternative sample, was based on largely pragmatic considerations. Nonetheless, it can be defended on several grounds. First, because University students are highly verbal, they can be expected to readily make the transition from real life to pencil and paper. Consequently, a set of paper and pencil responses constitutes a more representative sample of behavior for this group than it would for most other groups. Second, the undergraduate experience is psychologically rich. In Lewin's (1951) terms, many boundaries in the (still) adolescent life space remain only tentatively articulated; new regions in which achievement and exploration may be made are suddenly accessible. In Erikson's (1950) terms, problems of identity are being played out - or not played out - at this time more than at any other. Institutional pressures towards conformity, perhaps objectively less severe here than at later times in life, are perceived in a largely and meaningfully idiosyncratic fashion. The presence of this multiplicity serves to provide a broad range of feasible behaviors in many situations. Because of these concerns, the question

What would I do in this situation?

can typically be answered in more meaningfully disparate ways at this time than at most other points in the life span. For many reasons, college undergraduates remain a population deserving of study by personality psychologists (cf., Carlson, 1984).

5.1.2 The sample of situations

The present set of situations has been reduced from an initial pool of over 1,000 items which were provided by 39 University of California undergraduates in pretesting in the Fall of 1983. Subjects in this study were asked to choose one of a list of trait words and to monitor themselves over a period of three weeks by noting, each day, those behaviors and situations which they felt were indicative of the trait that they had chosen to monitor.

From this extensive list of situations, wholly redundant items have been removed, as well as improbable or overly specific situations, such as

I had just colored my hair and I was visiting a friend

as well as overly general ones, including

At school after class.

Most of the remaining situations have been rewritten to be more general, so that any student could imagine him or herself in that situation, and, further, so that variability would be obtained in behaviors endorsed by undergraduates. Most of the rewritten items have the same flavor as the items originally reported by students, as with this item which was altered to obtain grammatical coherence:

He did not know how to do.

-> *He did not know how to do his homework.*

Other items, typically edited to obtain conciseness or more (or occasionally less) generality, have probably lost something in the translation:

I had plans to meet my sister for lunch and she didn't show up. So I ate lunch by myself which I ended up enjoying because someone left the newspaper which I read. I was irritated because I told the waiter it would be a party for 2. I felt stupid (what a loser because my date dumped me) when it turned out to be only 1.

-> *Your friend shows up an hour late for a date.*

As can be seen in these examples, the rewritten situations are occasionally quite different from those originally supplied by students. Nonetheless, they are believed to be essentially similar in their psychological significance.

The current set of 102 situations appears, in all but one respect, to sample in a representative fashion from diverse aspects of undergraduate life. The exception is that the situations are typically more conflict-laden than those typically encountered by undergraduates. Consider, for example, the following two situations:

A friend calls and is upset or concerned.

A friend calls while you are studying and is upset or concerned.

In the first situation, the appropriate behavior is relatively unambiguous (i.e., help or listen to the person). As a result, the situation is highly constraining, and will be uninformative concerning differences between persons. In the second situation, an element of conflict is introduced, and helping the person now carries with it a cost (i.e., interruption of studying). The range of anticipated behaviors is, consequently, greater. The second situation, by virtue of the added element of conflict, is less constraining and more potentially diagnostic of personality variables of interest.

5.1.3 The sample of trait words

The behaviors of the SBI are scaled on five trait words, *achievement*, *conscientiousness*, *friendliness*, *irritability*, and *self- consciousness*. These trait words were chosen following several criteria.

The first criterion was that the trait words to be measured should be generally salient as well as interpersonally variable in the population being studied. The frequency of selection of trait words in the Fall, 1983 pretest was used as an index of salience. In that study, the most frequently chosen traits were *achievement orientation*, *thoughtfulness*, *playfulness*, *self-consciousness*, and *independence*.

The second criterion was that these trait words should provide continuity with prior studies. The prominence of Bem and Allen's (1974) study and the similarity of the present study to the objectives specified by Bem and Allen in their theoretical discussion virtually necessitates an inclusion of the two trait words they studied, conscientiousness and friendliness, in the present study. A similar argument can be made for the trait of hostility (see Chapter 4).

No attempt was made to include traits which were mutually orthogonal; indeed, the presence of correlated traits would allow examination of the role of scalability as a fine tool in distinguishing between normatively similar concepts. Nonetheless, it could be argued that the five trait words represent, more or less adequately, the five dimensions of observer ratings found by Tupes and Christal (1961): conscientiousness is close to Tupes and Christal's dependability, irritability is similar to agreeableness (albeit reversed), and self-consciousness is related to surgency (reversed) and emotional stability.

Friendliness appears related to Tupes and Christal's factors of agreeableness and surgency, and achievement-orientation is related to surgency, dependability, and culture. Some factors outside the Big Five factor space were also considered, such as masculinity-femininity (Lanning & Gough, 1990) and authoritarianism (Lanning, 1990).

From these initial criteria, trait words perceived to be largely - though, it is acknowledged, never entirely - redundant have been eliminated. Where two trait words had similar meanings but one was used only to label relatively extreme characteristics, the more moderate term was chosen. Thus, *Self-consciousness* is retained rather than anxiety; *Irritability* was similarly chosen over hostility. *Friendliness* was chosen over sociability, and *Conscientiousness* was chosen over thoughtfulness because of the primacy of the Bem and Allen study. *Achievement* was retained because of its obvious salience for the population of persons, behaviors, and situations to be examined. Working definitions of the five trait words are as follows:

Achievement is working hard to overcome obstacles or striving to do well in the pursuit of difficult and admirable goals. When people put in extra effort to attain these goals, their behavior is high on achievement. When people give up on or abandon goals, or act as if they don't have goals, their behavior is low on achievement.

Conscientiousness is being guided by principles, rules, and feelings of "should" or "ought to". When people act because of their principles, or act thoughtfully rather than doing what is easiest, their behavior is high on conscientiousness. When people do things without thinking about whether or not they should, their behavior is low on conscientiousness.

Friendliness is giving people attention, respect, encouragement, trust, and/or assistance. When people are open towards others, and act positively towards them, their behavior is high on friendliness. When people ignore other people, are distrusting, discouraging, disrespectful, or unhelpful, their behavior is low on friendliness.

Irritability is the tendency to be easily frustrated, and to show this frustration with impatience, intolerance, or anger. When people lose their tempers, act intolerant, or get impatient, their behavior is high on irritability. When people are relaxed, flexible, and patient, their behavior is low on irritability.

Self-consciousness is thinking about how other people perceive one's self. When people worry about how they are seen so much that they feel shy or embarrassed, their behavior is high on self-consciousness. When people behave openly, without worrying about how they are seen, their behavior is low on self-consciousness.

5.1.4 The sample of behaviors

For each of the situations of the SBI, subjects are asked to choose a single behavior. As the length of the list of behaviors increases, the amount of time necessary to complete the inventory increases proportionately, hence, the list of behaviors should be short. On the other hand, subjects must be able to choose a satisfactory behavior for each of the situations they encounter. If the set of situations is diverse (as in the SBI), this would tend to produce a long list of response options. The conflicting requirements are met, somewhat, by the inclusion of behaviors which are fairly general.

The behaviors reported by subjects in the Fall, 1983 exploratory study were combined into general behaviors or themes (e.g., *Work or study alone*). Behaviors were also obtained from Lamiell's (1982) set of college activities to provide a preliminary set of behaviors, and from a specification of behaviors believed to be high, moderate, and low on elevation for each of the five traits.

5.2 Iterative refinement of the SBI

In reducing the SBI to its present form, an iterative approach was used. Initial culling of the set of situations for non-redundant, general items led to a set of 203 items. For each of these, a list of plausible response options was constructed. Situations which called for relatively unique behaviors were eliminated (e.g., *A friend offers you a clove cigarette*). The remaining set of responses was combined with the preliminary set of behaviors; several behaviors were added at this point and others were consolidated in an attempt to provide an adequate (though brief) set of response options.

The resulting matrix was again inspected to insure that all plausible behaviors were among the available response options for each situation; two judges agreed that this requirement was met. Infrequently appropriate behaviors were then eliminated. This reduced set of behaviors was then re-examined against the set of situations; situations which called for absent or infrequent behaviors were eliminated. This process continued iteratively until a set of 152 situations and 28 behaviors was obtained. These 28 behaviors were rated by a sample of undergraduates on each of five trait words, as described in Section 5.3.

A number of staff members of the Institute of Personality Assessment and Research (IPAR) completed the inventory at this interim stage of development. Their comments suggested that the inventory was not yet ready for administration. Specifically, the list of behaviors was too long, and certain situations required behaviors not present on the list. Accordingly, 10 of the 28 behaviors were eliminated, as were the situations which called for these behaviors. At this point, the reduction of situations on purely formal grounds had resulted in the over-representation of certain types of situation and the under-representation of other types. Accordingly, certain redundant situations were dropped, and certain previously dropped situations were rephrased and added. This resulted in the present version of the inventory, which consists of 102 situations and 18 behaviors. The items or situations are provided in Appendix 1; the behaviors or response options are shown in Table 5.1.

The measure is, in its current form, not yet complete. The reduction of the set of behaviors to the present set of 18 has been severe, and has resulted in the lack of a perfect correspondence between "what subjects would in fact do" and the set of available response options. The resulting awkwardness is alleviated by instructions to subjects to choose the item which best matches their behavior. These instructions are included at the beginning of Appendix 1.

5.3 Scaling of behaviors

Subjects included 43 Male and 46 Female University of California undergraduates. These individuals were asked to provide Likert ratings of 28 behaviors on each of five trait words. By participating in the study, subjects satisfied a portion of the experimental credit requirement for the introductory psychology course in which they were enrolled.

Subjects completed the ratings in individual sessions; items were administered by microcomputer. Prior to providing the 140 ratings used in the determination of elevation scores, subjects rated 10 items in a warm-up period which allowed subjects to familiarize themselves with the response scale. These items were repeated at the end of the ratings. The computer keyboard was modified so that only the numeric keypad was visible; the remaining keys were covered by a board on which the definitions of the five trait words (see Section 5.1.3) were printed.

The presence of 10 repeated items permits examination of test- retest correlations. Examination of these correlations as a function of order of presentation suggests that subjects ratings became more stable as their familiarity with the task increased; at about the seventh item, the test-retest coefficients asymptote at approximately .50. The correlation between the 1st rating and the (identical) 141st was .16; the correlation between the 10th rating and the 150th was .51. Intermediate values were .40, .33, .18, .17, .23, .53, .50, and .51, respectively. (*Text continues on page 66*).

TABLE 5.1 - MEAN RATINGS OF 18 BEHAVIORS ON FIVE TRAIT WORDS

Mean	S.D.		Behavior	Sex difference
Achievement				
6.83	0.43	a	Persist, work until it is done or correct.	F > M
6.29	1.01	b	Take the initiative yourself.	
6.01	1.02	c	Ask why; get more information.	
5.94	0.97	c	Work or study (alone).	
5.65	1.10	d	Act responsibly; do the right thing.	
5.33	0.94	e	Help or cooperate with them.	
5.26	1.19	e	Ask (someone) for help.	
5.00	1.10	e	Remind them about what they should do.	
4.48	1.35	f	Get together with friends.	
4.42	1.44	f	Not take it personally; forget it.	
4.03	0.98	g	Do something flirtatious, romantic, or erotic.	
3.96	1.11	gh	Be frank and say you can't help them.	
3.90	1.27	gh	Take it personally; feel hurt.	
3.85	1.28	gh	Cry; express distress.	
3.84	1.41	gh	Get upset; express frustration.	
3.83	1.10	gh	Relax, rest, or take a break.	
3.73	1.02	h	Feel embarrassed, blush, or be tongue-tied.	
1.70	1.14	i	Give up, do something else.	
Conscientiousness				
6.21	1.29	a	Act responsibly; do the right thing.	
6.03	0.82	a	Persist, work until it is done or correct.	F > M
5.49	1.06	b	Help or cooperate with them.	F > M
5.39	1.28	b	Remind them about what they should do.	
5.26	1.25	bc	Ask why; get more information.	
5.02	1.26	c	Take the initiative yourself.	M > F
4.65	1.10	d	Work or study (alone)	
4.44	1.24	de	Feel embarrassed, blush, or be tongue-tied.	
4.42	1.35	de	Ask (someone) for help.	
4.37	1.06	e	Get together with friends.	
4.29	1.34	e	Take it personally; feel hurt.	
4.05	1.51	ef	Be frank and say you can't help them.	M > F
3.90	0.99	fg	Relax, rest, or take a break.	
3.63	1.68	gh	Not take it personally; forget it.	
3.49	1.33	h	Get upset; express frustration.	
3.36	1.60	h	Cry; express distress.	
3.29	1.29	h	Do something flirtatious, romantic, or erotic.	
2.71	1.16	i	Give up, do something else.	

(*Table continues*)

TABLE 5.1 - MEAN RATINGS OF 18 BEHAVIORS ON FIVE TRAIT WORDS (CONTINUED)

Mean	S.D.		Behavior	Sex difference
Friendliness				
6.46	0.81	a	Get together with friends.	
6.32	0.74	a	Help or cooperate with them.	
5.56	1.17	b	Do something flirtatious, romantic, or erotic.	
5.26	1.28	bc	Take the initiative yourself.	F > M
5.21	0.89	c	Ask (someone) for help.	
5.03	1.31	cd	Act responsibly; do the right thing.	F > M
4.97	0.96	cd	Ask why; get more information.	
4.90	1.66	cde	Not take it personally; forget it.	
4.83	1.22	de	Remind them about what they should do.	
4.54	0.93	ef	Relax, rest, or take a break.	
4.45	0.95	fg	Persist, work until it is done or correct.	
4.17	1.13	g	Cry; express distress.	
3.81	0.99	h	Feel embarrassed, blush, or be tongue-tied.	
3.57	1.52	hi	Be frank and say you can't help them.	M > F
3.51	1.00	i	Give up, do something else.	
3.45	1.34	i	Take it personally; feel hurt.	
3.19	1.28	ij	Get upset; express frustration.	
3.02	1.16	j	Work or study (alone)	
Irritability				
6.03	0.82	a	Get upset; express frustration.	
5.70	1.31	b	Give up, do something else.	
5.24	1.53	c	Cry; express distress.	
5.03	1.25	c	Take it personally; feel hurt.	
4.56	1.60	d	Be frank and say you can't help them.	
4.43	1.34	d	Work or study (alone)	
4.42	1.36	d	Remind them about what they should do.	
3.97	1.32	e	Feel embarrassed, blush, or be tongue-tied.	
3.90	1.53	e	Take the initiative yourself.	
3.45	1.14	f	Ask why; get more information.	
3.39	1.30	fg	Ask (someone) for help.	F > M
3.30	1.14	gh	Act responsibly; do the right thing.	
2.96	1.70	hi	Relax, rest, or take a break.	
2.90	1.46	i	Persist, work until it is done or correct.	
2.73	1.07	i	Get together with friends.	
2.65	1.41	i	Do something flirtatious, romantic, or erotic.	
2.18	1.39	j	Not take it personally; forget it.	
2.11	1.20	j	Help or cooperate with them.	

(Table continues)

Table 5.1 - Mean ratings of 18 behaviors on five trait words (continued)

Mean	S.D.		Behavior	Sex difference
Self-consciousness				
6.26	1.28	a	Feel embarrassed, blush, or be tongue-tied.	
5.48	1.67	b	Take it personally; feel hurt.	
4.57	1.43	c	Act responsibly; do the right thing.	
4.55	1.45	c	Persist, work until it is done or correct.	
4.30	1.39	cd	Work or study (alone)	
3.97	1.49	de	Help or cooperate with them.	
3.73	1.34	efg	Give up, do something else.	
3.66	1.60	efg	Get upset; express frustration.	
3.66	1.40	f	Get together with friends.	M > F
3.51	1.60	fgh	Ask (someone) for help.	
3.38	1.05	fgh	Relax, rest, or take a break.	
3.30	1.51	gh	Ask why; get more information.	
3.29	1.62	gh	Remind them about what they should do.	
3.18	1.76	hi	Cry; express distress.	
3.17	1.63	hi	Take the initiative yourself.	
3.16	1.59	hi	Be frank and say you can't help them.	
2.72	1.85	ij	Do something flirtatious, romantic, or erotic.	
2.64	1.63	j	Not take it personally; forget it.	

Note: N = 43 Males, 46 Females. Means sharing a common subscript are not significantly different at $p < .05$ (t-test for correlated means). Significant ($p < .05$) sex differences are indicated.

Mean ratings are shown in Table 5.1. For each trait, significance tests on all pairs of behaviors and sex differences in mean ratings (t-tests for correlated means and independent samples, respectively) are also provided. It will be recalled that these mean values provide estimates of behavioral elevation to be later used in the computation of scalability and elevation scores from the SBI.

Prior to consideration of the individual traits, some general comments may be made. The overall level of consensus as to the placement of items was not high; this was to be expected, as the heterogeneity of both the set of trait words and behaviors resulted in a number of strained behavior-trait pairs (e.g., *Take the initiative yourself* for *Irritability*). As a result, a number of the mean estimates for behaviors on each dimension have overlapping standard errors. Examination of Table 5.1 shows that, for each set of 18 behaviors, no more than nine to ten statistically separate means can be discerned. This suggests a moderate degree of ambiguity in the ratings of behaviors on these traits, and, consequently, the presence of substantial measurement error in the elevation and scalability measures which will later rely on these ratings.

The average rating, over behaviors, for the traits of *Achievement*, *Friendliness*, and *Conscientiousness* were near the midpoint (4.5) of the rating scale; these means were 4.67, 4.57, and 4.54, respectively. Means for the traits of *Irritability* (3.83) and *Self-consciousness* (3.81) were somewhat lower. The five vectors of mean ratings are not independent. The correlation, over 18 behaviors, between the average ratings on *Achievement* and the average ratings on *Conscientiousness* was .83; the corresponding figure for *Friendliness* and *Irritability* was - .78. These correlations provide a measure of the overlap of the different Elevation measures: the expected correlation, over persons, between the Elevation scores for any two traits will be equivalent to the correlation between the sets of means from which these scores are derived. The matrix of correlations between the five traits, over behaviors, is shown in Table 5.2.

Examination of the ratings of the behaviors on the individual traits in Table 5.1 shows that the mean ratings for the trait of *Achievement* describe task orientation at the high end, and a combination of passivity and emotionality at the low end of the scale. The (similar) *Conscientiousness* dimension taps rule-conscious, responsible behavior *versus* behaviors describing a lack of impulse control and a readiness to abandon projects. Friendliness is characterized by social, outgoing behaviors *versus* private, emotional activities. *Irritability*, similar to *Friendliness* (but reversed), describes negativism and emotionality *versus* cooperativeness and sociability. Finally, at the high end of the *Self-Consciousness* dimension are behaviors characterizing sensitivity and private emotionality, at the low end are behaviors describing an easy-going if somewhat shallow style of interaction.

A final comment should be made on the ratings. The present set of mean estimates of elevation depended, in part, on the context in which these ratings were made (Mellers & Birnbaum, 1982). Specifically, these ratings depend upon those behaviors which were dropped from the original set of 28 as well as those retained. The behavior *Work or study (alone)*, for example, was rated at the bottom of the *Friendliness* dimension. The rating for this behavior probably was depressed by the presence of other items, including *Work or*

TABLE 5.2: INTERCORRELATIONS, OVER BEHAVIORS, OF MEAN ELEVATION SCORES

	Con	Fre	Irr	Scn
Achievement	.83	.35	-.46	.01
Conscientiousness		.34	-.40	.32
Friendliness			-.78	-.34
Irritability				.17
Self- Consciousness				

Note: N = 18 behaviors. Con = Conscientiousness, Fre = Friendliness, Irr = Irritability, Scn = Self-consciousness.

study (with others). The remaining behaviors rated by subjects but not used in the SBI include the following:

Exercise; do something athletic.
Go off on your own, forget the others.
Avoid or reduce discord or friction.
Ask them to be considerate.
Laugh or do something silly.
Get angry; lose your temper.
Eat a lot of food.
Feel too nervous to act on the impulse.
Consume alcohol or drugs.

5.4 Summary

The development of the Situation Behavior Inventory (SBI) has been described. The measure is attractive in that it includes a diverse range of items (or situations) which sample from a wide spectrum of those that are germane to undergraduate life. However, the range of behaviors offered to subjects for each of these situations may not be adequate to allow all subjects to respond in an entirely natural manner in each of these. Conversely, in each of the situations, a number of the response options violate implicit social rules (Argyle, Furnham, & Graham, 1981). As a result, many of the resulting situation-behavior pairs are somewhat bizarre, such as

You need to get your homework done. A friend asks if you want to work with him or her. (Situation)
= > *Cry, express distress.* (Behavior)

It is possible that further work on the inventory could lead to a measure which remains representative of undergraduate life while providing a brief set of behaviors in each situation which is both sufficient to allow all subjects to respond naturally and necessary, in that each behavior would be chosen by some subjects in each situation.

Alternatively, the inventory could be improved by altering its form rather than its content. A change in the response format might be considered: subjects could, for example, be presented with a subset of a longer list of responses for each situation. Or, the response format could be changed from a simple list of possible behaviors to a hierarchically structured set of responses. Here, for each situation, subjects would first provide a general response, such as *Do something social*, followed by a more specific option, *Visit with one friend*.

Both of these changes have the apparent advantage, over the present format, of allowing for each item a wider range of behavioral possibilities, while not requiring the subject to consider irrelevant options. But these alternatives are each more complex than the present response format. This additional complexity will require subjects to in effect relearn the set of options for each item; consequently, subjects might take a longer period of time to become familiar with the set of responses than they would for a simple list. The relative efficiency of different response formats is an empirical question which, though worthy of examination, will not be examined in the present monograph.

It is likely that the major limitations of the SBI lie not with its content, but in its attempt to map a complex social world into a simple, formal system which implicitly (and incorrectly) treats behaviors and situations as orthogonal (Argyle et al., 1981). In any event, the usefulness of the SBI and its measures of scalability can best be assessed empirically, as will be done in the next chapter.

6

Scalability and Elevation as Measured by the SBI

The Situation Behavior Inventory (SBI) provides measures of Elevation and Scalability on five traits in a sample of University undergraduates. In the present chapter, an empirical investigation of the SBI and its various measures is described.

The research questions to be examined in this chapter parallel those cited previously in the examination of the Situational Hostility Scale in Chapter 4. These include, but are not limited to, the following:

How reliable are the measures?

To what extent is scalability independent of elevation?

Do different measures of scalability tap substantively different constructs?

What are the zero-order correlates of scalability measures?

Does scalability function as a moderator in the prediction of non-test measures from elevation?

Although no single study could provide definitive answers to all of these questions, the present investigation provides evidence relevant to each.

6.1 Methods

Subjects. The items of the SBI describe diagnostic situations likely to be encountered by University undergraduates (see Chapter 5). As such, the appropriate subject population was self-evident. The sample consists of 115 Male and 89 Female University of California undergraduates. These individuals received experimental credit for the introductory psychology courses in which they were enrolled.

Measures and procedures. In addition to the SBI, a number of validational measures were administered. Self-report measures included the California Psychological Inventory (CPI; Gough, 1975), the Adjective Check List (ACL; Gough & Heilbrun, 1983), and the Self-Consciousness Scale (Fenigstein, Scheier & Buss, 1975). Subjects also completed portions of several other inventories; these include the General Activity (G), Personal Relations (P), and Friendliness (F) scales of the Guilford-Zimmerman Temperament Survey (GZTS; Guilford, Guilford, & Zimmerman, 1978), and the Irritability scale of the Buss Durkee Hostility Inventory (Buss & Durkee, 1957). Most subjects also completed the Self-Monitoring Scale (Snyder, 1974) and a Role Construct Repertory (REP) Grid (Kelly, 1963). In addition, subjects were asked to rate each of the five trait words on three dimensions. These were Elevation (how characteristic the trait word was of the person), Consistency (how consistent they were with respect to the trait word), and Importance (how important the trait word was for the person). These self-report measures, with the exception of the ACL and the REP grid, were administered by computer in groups of 3 to 12 subjects. Administration was in two sessions separated by one week; the total time required for the computer sessions was approximately 165 minutes.

On the REP grid, subjects were asked to choose, from a set of supplied constructs, those which best distinguished between sets of three individuals. Subjects were encouraged to use their own constructs where none of the supplied dimensions were adequate. The supplied constructs included eleven dimensions. These are listed below:

Achieving versus lazy
Attractive versus unattractive
Conscientious versus irresponsible
Dependent versus independent
Friendly versus aloof
Irritable versus easy going
Masculine versus feminine
Open minded versus closed minded
Playful versus serious
Rational versus emotional
Self conscious versus un-self conscious

For the REP grid, subjects were asked to describe the following eight target persons: Self, Mother, Father, High school friend, New friend, an Admired person, a Pitied person, and Someone who liked the subject.

Several measures were taken from outside of the traditional self- report domain. In the interim week between computer sessions, subjects completed, on a daily basis, a form reporting the frequency or duration of a number of activities and emotions believed relevant to the set of traits presently studied. Included in these *behavior logs* were questions asking subjects how many hours they spent alone, with friends, with family, studying, in class, and on other duties. In addition, subjects noted the number of times they felt bored, embarrassed, nervous, happy, sociable, confident, and irritated. Subjects also reported whether or not they had missed any appointments or classes, and whether or not they had arrived late for appointments or classes. Subjects were encouraged to complete the behavior log each night before retiring. In an effort to reduce retrospective completion of these forms, subjects were instructed as follows:

> *If you miss a night, you should leave the section blank rather than go back and try to remember the information.*

Finally, each subject was provided with a second ACL and set of ratings, together with instructions and a stamped envelope. Subjects were instructed to give these packets to "someone who knows you well".

Most, but not all, subjects completed all of the measures. The number of male and female subjects for whom data are available on each measure is summarized in Table 6.1.

TABLE 6.1: MEASURES AND NUMBERS OF CASES

Data type Measure	Males	Females
Self report inventories		
Situation Behavior Inventory	115	89
California Psychological Inventory	115	89
Guilford Zimmerman Temperament Survey[a]	115	89
Buss Durkee Hostility Inventory[a]	115	89
Self Monitoring Scale	81	62
Other self report measures		
Self Adjective Check List	113	87
Self ratings	115	89
Role Construct Repertory Grid	111	86
Daily Behavior log Form	111	86
Peer measures		
Peer ratings	72	49
Peer Adjective Check List	78	54

[a]Not all items administered

6.2 Scoring and scale construction

For each trait, the responses to the SBI were recoded using the mean ratings of Table 5.1. Each trait was then scored separately using the Pascal computer program in Appendix 2. This program accepts as input any rectangular matrix with numerical entries, and returns a residual matrix and two files describing marginal scores. The residual matrix may be thought of as the data file of scalability items. Where the input file is a person (row) by item (column) matrix, the two marginal files describe person (elevation, scalability) and item (evocativeness, average residual) statistics.

Several approaches to scoring scalability were considered.

Unreduced scales. First, scalability and elevation scores were computed from the matrices of all 102 items and 204 subjects. (There were five such matrices, one for each of the traits in the previous chapter).

It will be recalled that scalability scores for any single individual depend, in part, on the scores obtained by other individuals (as represented by the item evocativeness and overall mean scores in Equation 2). Because of this, scalability scores computed on the entire sample were compared to scores computed on separate matrices for each sex. The correlation between the scalability measures computed within-sex and the measures computed on the combined sample was .99 or greater for all five measures. This provides some encouraging evidence concerning the robustness of scalability scores over changes in sample characteristics; more to the point, the similarity of the combined-sex analyses to the within-sex analyses allows all of the remaining computations of scalability scores to be based on the combined sample.

Internally consistent scales. Loevinger (1957) has noted the tension between *classical* and *scaling* approaches to test construction.

The classical approach selects items based on their corrected part-whole correlations; those items with the highest correlations are then retained for inclusion in a scale. Because the correlation coefficient is sensitive to differences in the distributions of the variables being compared, this approach typically leads to a set of items which are similar in evocativeness or difficulty. Items selected to maximize the scalability of a measure, on the other hand, will be widely different in their difficulties.

For example, the ordering of the items

8 + 12 = ? and

11 - 3 = ?

in a sample of third graders will be less stable than the ordering of the items

1 + 1 = ? and

12 X 9 = ?

in the same sample of persons. By this same logic, individual differences in scalability for persons will be most stable when the items differ greatly in evocativeness or difficulty. Conversely, scalability scores computed on an internally consistent set of items which is homogeneous in difficulty will be relatively error-laden.

But it is possible that this hypothetical limitation on the potential utility of item analysis for measures of scalability can be sidestepped, simply by building scales based on the internal consistency of the residual as well as the raw scores. Accordingly, for each trait, internally homogeneous scales were constructed by inspecting the corrected item-total correlations of both the elevation and the scalability measures. For each trait, items with part-whole correlations less than approximately .10 in either measure were screened out. This threshold was not met by numerous scalability items and somewhat fewer elevation items. The responses to the best 30 items for each trait were then resubmitted to the scalability program. This last step is necessary because simply totalling and reversing the previously computed residual scores would not provide a true index of scalability, but would reflect dropped items as well.

Scales consisting of non-extreme items. Opposing the argument that items should be dispersed in difficulty to maximize scalability is the counter-argument that a scale consisting of items which are widely variable in difficulty will include extreme items, and extreme items are more susceptible to the problem of entailment which we have repeatedly encountered.

In light of this argument, I constructed scales consisting entirely of non-extreme items. Here, items were considered extreme if the average response, over subjects, fell outside of the inter-quartile range of response options. Scalability scores were then recomputed on these reduced scales.

Internally consistent and non-extreme scales. An additional scale construction approach combined the two methods of the preceding sections. I performed an item analysis on the non-extreme scales, in the hopes of combining the hypothetical virtues of the internal consistency and non-extreme scale strategies described in the preceding paragraphs.

Altogether, these approaches led to four measures of scalability and four measures of elevation for each of the five traits. Again, these major approaches to scale construction were (a) scales based on the entire set of 102 items, (b) scales consisting of internally consistent items, (c) scales consisting of non-extreme items, and (d) scales consisting of items which were both internally-consistent and non-extreme.

Additional scale construction techniques. Several additional scale construction techniques were briefly examined. An attempt to compute smoothed measures of scalability by aggregating over items similar in evocativeness (see Chapter 4) led to measures which were not reliable. (The median, over the five traits, of the best lower bound reliability estimates was .26). It is probable that a more content-laden approach to aggregating items would lead to better results.

Finally, rationally developed measures were based on the estimates of five IPAR judges as to the diagnosticity of the situations for the traits. These measures were only slightly more reliable than the smoothed measures (median reliability = .47). Further explorations into the properties of the smoothed and rational measures were not undertaken.

Scoring of target measures. For each of the five traits, I constructed three composite target variables. These target variables are intended to serve as validational measures for the SBI scales, and, further, will function as "criteria" for assessing the utility of scalability in moderated multiple regression analyses. These targets were derived from three different data sources, peer adjectives, self-report inventories, and the daily behavior logs, and are shown in Table 6.2.

The behavior logs were scored by averaging, for each individual, over all non-missing days. REP grids were scored as to the presence versus absence of the traits of *achievement, conscientiousness, friendliness, irritability,* and *self-consciousness*.

TABLE 6.2: COMPOSITE TARGET VARIABLES

	Achievement	Conscientiousness	Friendliness	Irritability	Self-Consciousness
Peer ACL clusters					
+	Ambitious	Civilized	Cheerful	Hostile	Anxious
	Industrious	Conscientious	Friendly	Impatient	Awkward
	Intelligent	Dependable	Good-natured	Irritable	Deliberate
	Persevering	Fair-minded	Outgoing	Mischievous	Nervous
	Rational	Honest	Sociable	Sarcastic	Sensitive
	Serious	Reliable	Understanding	Stubborn	Shy
	Thorough	Responsible	Warm	Temperamental	Worrying
-	Distractible	Absent-minded	Aloof	Apathetic	Assertive
	Dreamy	Careless	Arrogant	Calm	Energetic
	Easy-going	Deceitful	Cold	Contented	Flirtatious
	Lazy	Forgetful	Conceited	Indifferent	Frank
	Pessimistic	Irresponsible	Defensive	Fault-finding	Natural
	Quitting	Selfish	Distrustful	Relaxed	Outspoken
	Slipshod	Spontaneous	Self-centered	Obliging	Sophisticated
Self report clusters					
	CPI Ai	CPI Re	CPI Sy	CPI Sp	-CPI Sa
	CPI Cs	CPI So	CPI To		SCS Soc Anx
	GZTS G	GZTS P	GZTS F	BDHI I	SCS Pub SC
Behavior log clusters					
	Hours studied	Hours studied	Hours with friends	Irritated	Hours alone
	-Bored	Hours other duties	Friendly	Frustrated	Embarrassed
		-Late appts.	Happy	Angry	-Confident
		-Missed appts.		Afraid	

Note: CPI = California Psychological Inventory (1986 Revision). Ai - Achievement via Independence, Cs Capacity for Status, Re - Responsibility, So - Socialization, To - Tolerance, Sp -Social Presence, Sa - Self Acceptance. GZTS: Guilford Zimmerman Temperament Survey. G - General activity, P - Personal relations, F - Friendliness. BDHI I: Buss Durkee Hostility Inventory irritability. SCS: Self Consciousness Scale. Soc Anx - Social anxiety. Pub SC -Public Self-consciousness. ACL: Adjective Check List.

6.3 Results - Internal analyses

The results will be presented in some detail in two sections. First, internal analyses will be described, including descriptive statistics, reliabilities, and intercorrelations among the SBI measures. Following this, external results will be considered, including zero-order and higher-order correlations relating the SBI scales to the various target measures.

6.3.1 Descriptive statistics

The frequencies of the 20,808 simple responses to the SBI items are shown in Figure 6.1. The relative frequencies of the responses could not be accounted for by a single dimension of psychological content or social desirability. The most frequent responses were the following:

Help or cooperate with them
Get upset; express frustration

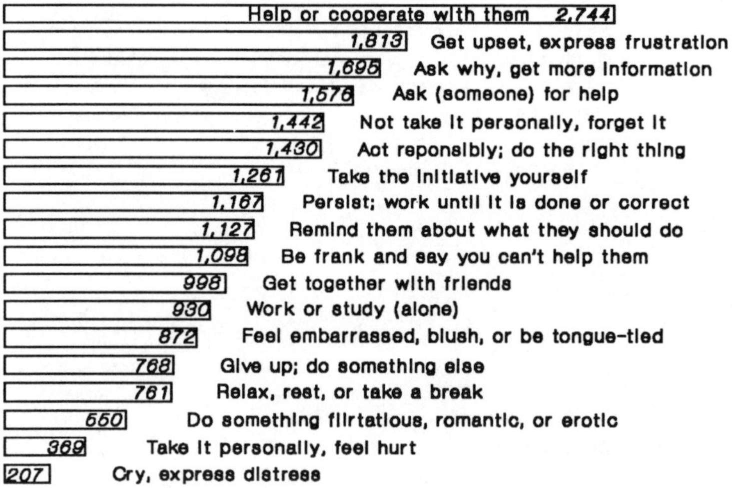

Figure 6.1: Frequencies of SBI responses, aggregated over persons and items.

The least frequent responses appeared more similar, describing negative emotional states:

Cry; express distress

Take it personally, feel hurt

In Figure 6.2, these same responses are presented individually for each of the five trait words. Descriptive statistics for these distributions are also provided. Gaps in these distributions reflect the absence of response options with elevation scores in the corresponding range (e.g., low to slightly low *Achievement*, low *Friendliness*).

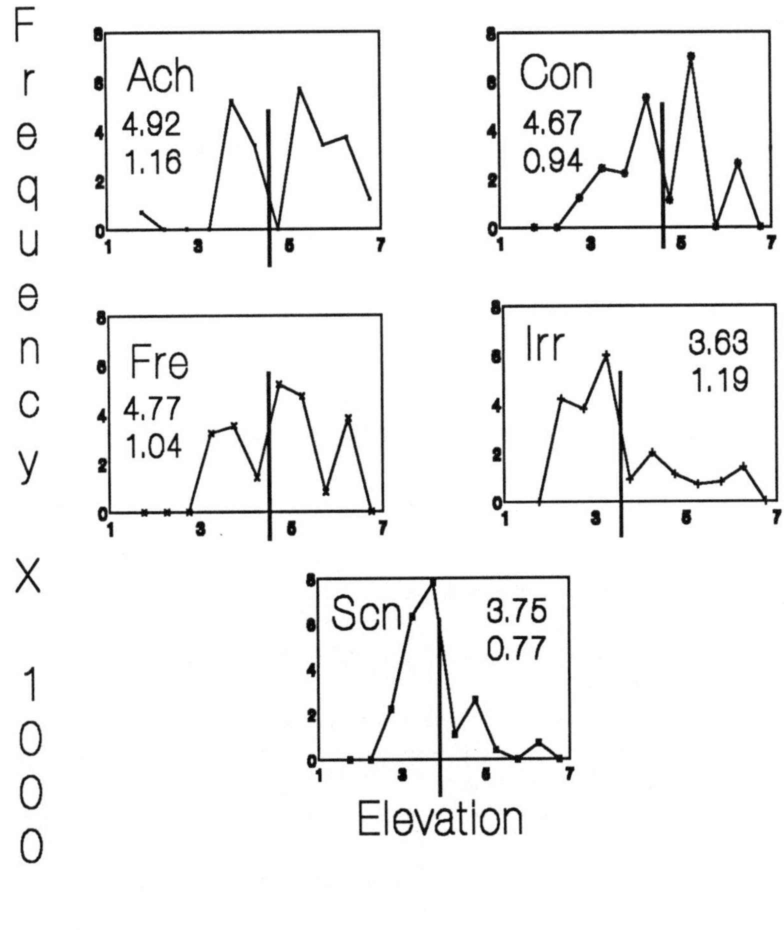

Figure 6.2: Distributions of SBI responses by elevation value and by trait, with means and standard deviations.

Figure 6.2 also reveals that the most frequently endorsed responses were high on Achievement, moderately high on *Friendliness* and *Conscientiousness*, and low on *Irritability* and *Self-consciousness*. The distributions for these last two variables display a moderate positive skew.

When the responses are scaled for each trait, the situations may be scored as to their evocativeness (or difficulty). The most and least evocative situations for each trait are shown in Table 6.3. *(Text continues on page 80).*

TABLE 6.3: MOST AND LEAST EVOCATIVE SITUATIONS FOR EACH TRAIT

Achievement - Most evocative situations

The instructor or teaching assistant gives you an unfair lab grade. (Item 32)

You land at the airport and are deciding how to get home. (41)

In a seminar, another student contradicts you but you are sure that you are right. (65)

You and another student had agreed to each summarize half of the readings for a class that you take together. You are supposed to meet to exchange notes the next day, but you haven't yet done the work. (73)

Just as you are turning in your homework assignment, you find a minor error that had been overlooked. (76)

Achievement - Least evocative situations

You have been working on a difficult homework problem all day. (10)

Some friends are having difficulties. You are discussing this with another friend, but this friend doesn't appreciate the gravity or seriousness of the situation. (69)

You need to do your Computer Science homework, but the computer has been 'down' for hours. (74)

You stumble on the steps in the lecture hall. (78)

You go to a movie, but upon arriving at the theater you realize that you don't have enough money for a ticket. (82)

Conscientiousness - Most evocative situations

In a seminar, another student contradicts you but you are sure that you are right. (65)

You have an important exam coming up. A friend who is confused about the material asks for help. (66)

You and another student had agreed to each summarize half of the readings for a class that you take together. You are supposed to meet to exchange notes the next day, but you haven't yet done the work. (73)

Just as you are turning in your homework assignment, you find a minor error that had been overlooked. (76)

You are supposed to attend a meeting, but have your own work as well. (95)

(Table continues)

TABLE 6.3: MOST AND LEAST EVOCATIVE SITUATIONS FOR EACH TRAIT (CONTINUED)

Conscientiousness - Least evocative situations

You don't like your new haircut. (68)

Some friends are having difficulties. You are discussing this with another friend, but this friend doesn't appreciate the gravity or seriousness of the situation. (69)

You need to do your Computer Science homework, but the computer has been 'down' for hours. (74)

A friend is helping you with homework and says something flirtatious. (81)

You go to a movie, but upon arriving at the theater you realize that you don't have enough money for a ticket. (82)

Friendliness - Most evocative situations

A friend asks you to drive him or her to the city to do some shopping. (6)

A friend asks to 'look at' the math or science homework that you have just completed. (36)

An acquaintance asks to borrow your registration card in order to go swimming on campus. (50)

You have an important exam coming up. A friend who is confused about the material asks for help. (66)

A friend calls while you are studying and is upset or concerned. (88)

Friendliness - Least evocative situations

Your parents tell their friends that you are interested in their son or daughter. (21)

You are working on a project with another student; the student makes a mistake and lets people believe that it was your fault. (26)

The instructor or assistant loses your best paper and doesn't even believe that you completed the assignment. (29)

You are trying to study at the library but it is too noisy. (46)

A friend says that you cheated in a game and you didn't. (51)

Irritability - Most evocative situations

You are working on a project with another student; the student makes a mistake and lets people believe that it was your fault. (26)

The instructor or assistant loses your best paper and doesn't even believe that you (29) completed the assignment.

You are trying to study at the library but it is too noisy. (46)

You need to do your Computer Science homework, but the computer has been 'down' for hours.(74)

Your roommates are noisy during finals week. (97)

(Table continues)

TABLE 6.3: MOST AND LEAST EVOCATIVE SITUATIONS FOR EACH TRAIT (CONTINUED)

Irritability - Least evocative situations

A friend asks you to drive him or her to the city to do some shopping. (6)

A friend asks to 'look at' the math or science homework that you have just completed. (36)

An acquaintance asks to borrow your registration card in order to go swimming on (50) campus.

You have an important exam coming up. A friend who is confused about the material asks for help. (66)

A friend calls while you are studying and is upset or concerned. (88)

Self-Consciousness - Most evocative situations

Your parents tell their friends that you are interested in their son or daughter. (21)

You are looking at an attractive person of the opposite sex and the person looks back at you.(58)

You and another student had agreed to each summarize half of the readings for a class that you take together. You are supposed to meet to exchange notes the next day, but you haven't yet done the work.(73)

You stumble on the steps in the lecture hall. (78)

It is your first time in the exercise class or weight room. (100)

Self-Consciousness - Least evocative situations

Someone scratches one of your phonograph records. (1)

The garbage needs to be taken out, but it is someone else's responsibility. (2)

Somebody tries to sneak in line ahead of you in the administration building. (30)

A friend throws ice down your shirt. (63)

You and your roommates are going to have a party but they aren't helping in the preparations. (72)

The four scale construction techniques, two scoring methods, and five traits multiply to produce 40 SBI measures. Evidently, the measures are highly mutually dependent. Descriptive statistics for these measures are provided in Table 6.4. The last column indicates that the four different scale construction techniques resulted in measures that were highly intercorrelated. The remaining columns reveal additional findings. Among these it can be noted that the removal of extreme items lowered elevation scores on the traits of Achievement, Conscientiousness, and Friendliness, and raised these scores for the traits of Irritability and Self-consciousness. Females were marginally more elevated than males on Self-consciousness; females were more scalable than males for the traits of Conscientiousness and Irritability, but this was reversed for Self-consciousness. Finally, the selection of items which were internally consistent in both elevation and scalability resulted in consistent *increases* in the standard deviations of the distributions of person scores; this is the opposite of what is anticipated when scale reduction is made on the basis of correlations among elevation items alone.

TABLE 6.4: DESCRIPTIVE STATISTICS FOR 40 SBI SCALES

Scale / Sex	All items Mean	All items S.D.	Internally consistent Mean	Internally consistent S.D.	Non-extreme Mean	Non-extreme S.D.	Consistent & non-extreme Mean	Consistent & non-extreme S.D.	Median r^a
ELEVATION MEASURES									
Achievement									
Males	4.91	.20	4.98	.31	4.83	.20	4.80	.32	.86
Females	4.93	.24	5.03	.34	4.85	.25	4.83	.33	.88
Conscientiousness									
Males	4.65	.18	4.68	.23	4.58	.18	4.56	.34	.84
Females	4.68	.21	4.75	.28	4.62	.22	4.61	.27	.92
Friendliness									
Males	4.77	.18	4.79	.28	4.68	.18	4.65	.28	.86
Females	4.75	.17	4.79	.27	4.65	.18	4.63	.27	.85
Irritability									
Males	3.61	.21	3.91	.38	3.80	.24	3.99	.39	.88
Females	3.64	.21	3.92	.38	3.84	.24	3.98	.40	.89
Self-consciousness									
Males	3.74	.12	3.63	.23	3.83	.13	3.76	.24	.87
Females	3.78*	.11	3.71*	.22	3.89*	.13	3.84*	.26	.84
SCALABILITY MEASURES									
Achievement									
Males	-0.75	.08	-0.80	.16	-0.75	.08	-0.81	.17	.81
Females	-0.73	.08	-0.77	.17	-0.73	.08	-0.79	.15	.80
Conscientiousness									
Males	-0.66*	.07	-0.68*	.14	-0.67*	.07	-0.67	.14	.87
Females	-0.63	.06	-0.64	.11	-0.65	.06	-0.64	.11	.80
Friendliness									
Males	-0.71	.09	-0.68	.17	-0.72	.09	-0.68	.15	.85
Females	-0.70	.08	-0.65	.14	-0.71	.08	-0.65	.14	.75
Irritability									
Males	-0.83	.11	-0.91*	.20	-0.88*	.12	-0.93*	.20	.86
Females	-0.80	.11	-0.85	.19	-0.84	.12	-0.86	.19	.88
Self-consciousness									
Males	-0.50	.07	-0.53	.17	-0.52	.07	-0.60	.16	.80
Females	-0.50	.07	-0.58*	.18	-0.52	.07	-0.66*	.18	.85

[a]Median correlations among the four scales in the row.

*$p < .05$ (Males - Females)

6.3.2 Reliabilities

Reliability estimates are shown in Table 6.5. These reliabilities (Guttman's Lambda 2 or Lambda 4) are lower bound estimates which are slightly (.00 to .07) higher than corresponding alpha reliabilities.

Among the elevation measures, the internally consistent measures are less consistent than the longer scales: It will be recalled that most items were rejected because of their failure to correlate with scalability, not elevation, and the elevation measures therefore failed to benefit from this technique. The non-extreme scales were slightly less reliable than the unselected measures. Reliabilities were highest for the Conscientiousness and Achievement scales, and somewhat lower for the Self-consciousness scale.

Among the scalability measures, the internally consistent measures were slightly more reliable than the longer measures; the non-extreme scales were also slightly less reliable than the longer measures. The Irritability scales were the highest, and the Achievement reliabilities were the lowest. All of these measures, however, appeared at least moderately reliable.

6.3.3 Relations between scalability and elevation (Entailment)

In the last two columns of Table 6.5, correlations between corresponding elevation and scalability measures are provided. Both linear and non-linear (quadratic and cubic) relations are summarized. The higher order multiples of elevation added little to the prediction of scalability; however, simple linear entailment was quite severe for three of the five traits (Friendliness, Irritability, and Self-Consciousness).

These correlations, describing the entailment of scalability scores by elevation, are reduced only slightly by the exclusion of extreme items. Entailment is exacerbated by the use of internally consistent items. Particularly troubling is the apparent correspondence between the column of reliabilities of the scalability measures and the columns of entailment values - using the last column as the best index of entailment, the correlation between the two vectors is .80. This suggests that much of the reliable variance in scalability scores may be due to their confounding with the more traditional measures.

6.3.4 Comparison of scale construction techniques

Careful examination of the reliabilities and correlations shown in Table 6.5 suggests that the differences among the various approaches to scale construction are, on the whole, modest. Consequently, in an appeal to

TABLE 6.5: RELIABILITIES AND CORRELATIONS BETWEEN SBI ELEVATION AND SCALABILITY MEASURES

	Length	Reliabilities		Entailment	
		Elevation	Scalability	r_{es}	$R_{s.e,e^2,e^3}$
Achievement					
All items	102	.81	.52	.26	.27
Int. consist.	30	.66	.60	.42	.47
Non-extreme	94	.81	.53	.14	.15
Int. consist.	30	.67	.57	.14	.17
Conscientiousness					
All items	102	.84	.66	.02	.09
Int. consist.	30	.67	.61	-.01	.02
Non-extreme	94	.84	.64	-.10	.10
Int. consist.	30	.66	.61	-.37	.38
Friendliness					
All items	102	.78	.73	.63	.65
Int. consist.	30	.74	.77	.78	.86
Non-extreme	90	.74	.71	.54	.57
Int. consist.	30	.71	.76	.75	.84
Irritability					
All items	102	.78	.80	-.70	.71
Int. consist.	30	.73	.75	-.70	.76
Non-extreme	82	.77	.76	-.58	.60
Int. consist.	30	.74	.75	-.64	.73
Self-Consciousness					
All items	102	.73	.69	-.64	.64
Int. consist.	30	.64	.77	-.88	.89
Non-extreme	79	.66	.58	-.52	.54
Int. consist.	30	.67	.78	-.84	.84

Note: N = 204. For reliability coefficients, the best lower bound estimates (Guttman's Lambda 2 or 4) are provided. By "entailment" is meant the relation between elevation and scalability.

brevity, it is appropriate to choose a single approach to scale construction for examination in the analyses which follow.

If there is a "best" approach to scale construction, at least insofar as entailment and reliability are concerned, it would appear to be the technique resulting in the scales consisting of non-extreme items. Given the inherent confounding present in extreme items, excluding these will provide a more powerful test of the potential contribution of this measurement approach. The remaining analyses will investigate only the scales consisting of non-extreme items. (Items composing these scales are included at the end of Appendix 1). The key results of analyses based on the non-reduced, 102-item scales are available elsewhere (Lanning, 1988); these are essentially similar to the present results.

Correlations among non-extreme scales. Table 6.6 shows the correlations among the measures consisting only of non-extreme items. These scales ranged in length from 79 to 94 items.

Among the elevation measures, Achievement and Conscientiousness appear similar as do Friendliness and reversed Irritability. These relations could have been anticipated on the basis of the similarity of the underlying behavior scales (see Table 5.2). Similar, though less extreme confounding exists with the scalability counterparts of these measures. Further inspection of this matrix reveals that for both sexes, the measures of Friendliness scalability and Irritability scalability correlated strongly with all of the traditional (Elevation) measures except for Self-Consciousness.

Two conclusions may be drawn from these internal analyses. First, the measures of scalability are reliable, but this reliable variance may not be unique. Secondly, strong relations among the measures of elevation underscore the interdependencies among these measures.

TABLE 6.6: INTERCORRELATIONS AMONG SBI MEASURES[a]

	Elevation					Scalability				
	Ach	Con	Fre	Irr	Scn	Ach	Con	Fre	Irr	Scn
Elevation measures										
Ach		.86	.54	-.63	-.06	.09	.14	.56	.71	.04
Con	.94		.54	-.59	.26	.04	-.07	.61	.73	-.11
Fre	.74	.72		-.86	-.26	.33	.25	.51	.57	.20
Irr	-.75	-.74	-.85		.20	-.28	-.18	-.54	-.58	.04
Scn	-.02	.17	-.13	-.01		-.10	-.16	-.04	.06	-.52
Scalability measures										
Ach	.19	.22	.15	-.15	.13		.55	.20	.20	.01
Con	-.01	-.17	.08	.01	-.10	.28		.10	.30	.18
Fre	.62	.62	.61	-.61	-.11	.26	-.09		.78	.01
Irr	.82	.84	.62	-.63	.15	.25	.03	.72		.03
Scn	.11	.05	.24	-.02	-.54	.02	.12	-.04	-.01	

Note: N = 115 Males (correlations above the diagonal), 89 Females (correlations below the diagonal). Ach - Achievement. Con - Conscientiousness. Fre - Friendliness. Irr - Irritability. Scn - Self-Consciousness.

[a] Scales consisting of non-extreme items.

6.4 Results - External analyses

From a practical standpoint, the utility of scalability lies in its role in predicting various non-test criteria. In this section, the zero-order correlates of the SBI scales will first be considered. Following this, moderated multiple regression analyses to predict the sets of target measures will be described.

6.4.1 Zero-order correlates of SBI measures

In Table 6.7, correlations between SBI measures and the other indices are shown. To conserve space, only statistically significant relations are presented. It should be stressed that these analyses are intended to be exploratory, and the results should be considered tentative. The reader is urged to recognize that the large number of statistical tests virtually guarantees that many results will attain the arbitrary .05 threshold purely by chance.

Elevation. The focus of the present investigation is scalability, not elevation, and so it might seem appropriate to bypass discussion of these correlations. But significant correlations between these measures and the target measures are necessary if the labels *Achievement*, *Conscientiousness*, and so forth are to have meaning. Accordingly, the correlations between the elevation measures and the target indices constitute evidence of the validity of the basic scales.

For four of the five trait words, elevation was significantly correlated with one or more target measures in both sexes. For the fifth trait word, *Irritability*, these "validity coefficients" ranged from only .05 to .16. This failure may be due to either the set of target measures for this trait, the elevation measure itself, or some combination of these. Regardless, without evidence of validity, this measure cannot be considered a measure of irritability, but remains instead a "measure x" of unknown significance.

We can do better than "measure x," of course, by examining the statistically significant zero-order correlates of the elevation and scalability measures of this trait in Table 6.7. In males, the strongest correlations included negative correlations with inventory measures of achievement (CPI Achievement via conformance and Achievement via independence), and peer ratings of conscientiousness (not Disorderly, indifferent). In females, the strongest correlates, again negative, were with the CPI validity scales (Good impression), and peer ratings of agreeableness (not Sulky, resentful, dissatisfied). The net picture is one of *cynicism* and *rebellion* rather than the intended content of low level permeability, disagreeableness, and irritability. (*Text continues on page 95*).

TABLE 6.7: SIGNIFICANT CORRELATES OF SBI MEASURES

			ACHIEVEMENT			
Elevation						
Males						
Target measures						
.37 Inventory composite						
CPI & Other inventory scales						
.27 Do	.46 Cs	.32 Sy	.32 Sa	.32 In	.34 Em	.33 Re
.22 So	.31 Gi	.31 Cm	.34 Wb	.29 To	.49 Ac	.33 Ai
.34 Ie	.26 Py	-.23 V1	.22 V2	.32 V3	-.23 S Anx	.20 G F
.22 G P						
Self ratings						
.26 Ach elevation		-.23 Ach variability		.21 Con elevation		
-.30 Con variability		-.20 Fre variability				
REP Grid/behavior report						
-.37 Attractive vs. unattractive				-.23 Times bored		
Peer ratings						
.25 Friendliness						
Peer ACL						
.30 Active		.28 High strung		.26 Mannerly		
.25 Stolid		-.25 Cowardly		-.27 Indifferent		
-.24 Submissive						
Females						
Target measures						
.35 Inventory composite						
CPI & other inventory scales						
.31 Do	.34 Cs	.24 Sy	.38 In	.22 Em	.29 Re	.27 So
.30 Sc	.49 Gi	.31 Wb	.24 To	.26 Ac	.33 Ie	.32 Py
-.30 Fe	-.23 V1	.24 V2	.36 V3	-.21 Pv S-C	-.28 Pb S-C	
-.34 S Anx	-.41 Sum S-C	-.26 B I	.26 G G			
Self ratings						
.25 Con elevation		-.21 Con variability				
REP Grid/behavior report						
-.23 Emotional vs. rational				-.24 Times nervous		
Peer ratings						
-.34 Dependence						
Peer ACL						
.28 Undependable		-.31 Dependent		-.31 Emotional		
-.27 Inhibited		-.29 Nervous		-.33 Thorough		
-.27 Sentimental		-.34 Timid		-.30 Vindictive		
-.40 Witty						

(Table continues)

TABLE 6.7: SIGNIFICANT CORRELATES OF SBI MEASURES (CONTINUED)

ACHIEVEMENT

Scalability
  Males
    CPI & other inventory scales
      .20 Do   .22 Sy   .25 Sa
    Self ratings
      .28 Fre elevation
    REP Grid
      -.20 Closed vs. open minded
    Peer ratings
      -.25 Open-minded   -.26 Self-conscious consistency
    Peer ACL

-.26 Withdrawn	.23 Loud	.25 Meek
.29 Outgoing	.23 Zany	-.23 Determined
-.24 Efficient	-.28 Forgiving	-.23 Good-looking
-.28 Imaginative	-.28 Individualistic	-.24 Organized
-.40 Persevering	-.28 Persistent	-.23 Progressive
-.24 Self-pitying	-.28 Serious	-.25 Slow
-.24 Tolerant	-.23 Unassuming	
-.29 Unconventional	-.23 Unstable	

  Females
    CPI & other inventory scales
      .22 V2   -.22 G G
    Self ratings
      .21 Fre importance
    REP Grid
      .27 Masculine vs. feminine
    Behavior report
      .22 Time bored
    Peer ACL and ratings

.34 Obliging	.38 Quarrelsome	.33 Robust
.31 Smug	-.27 Silent	
-.30 Conscientious (rating)		

CONSCIENTIOUSNESS

Elevation
  Males
    Target measures
      .33 Inventory composite   .23 Peer cluster   .21 Behavior cluster
    CPI & other inventory scales

.23 Cs	.33 Re	.25 So	.24 Sc	.37 Gi	.29 Cm	.24 Wb
.43 Ac	.35 V2	.20 V3	-.20 Pv S-C	-.18 B I	.23 G F	

(Table continues)

TABLE 6.7: SIGNIFICANT CORRELATES OF SBI MEASURES (CONTINUED)

CONSCIENTIOUSNESS

Elevation

- Males
  - *Self ratings*
    - .20 Ach elevation; -.23 Ach variability; .22 Con ele
    - -.23 Con variability; -.22 Fre variability
  - *REP Grid*
    - -.39 Attractive vs. unattractive; .23 *N* elicited constructs
  - *Behavior report*
    - -.26 Times late for class/appt.; -.20 Times bored
  - *Peer ACL*
    - .25 Active; .29 Cold; .24 Courageous
    - .24 Efficient; .23 Mannerly; .28 Organized
    - .23 Prudish; .31 Queer; .26 Stable
    - .26 Stern; .27 Stingy; .35 Stolid
    - -.26 Cowardly; -.32 Indifferent; -.25 Rebellious
    - -.29 Reckless; -.30 Rude; -.23 Submissive
- Females
  - *Target measures*
    - .36 Inventory composite
  - *CPI & other inventory scales*
    - .29 Do; .30 Cs; .33 In; .23 Em; .35 Re; .33 So; .36 Sc
    - .52 Gi; .29 Wb; .26 To; .32 Ac; .29 Ie; .27 Py; -.26 Fe
    - -.19 V1; .30 V2; .36 V3; -.22 Pv S-C; -.23 Pb S-C; -.29 S Anx
    - -.37 Sum S-C; -.30 B I; .26 G G
  - *Self ratings*
    - .23 Con elevation
  - *REP Grid*
    - -.22 Aloof vs. friendly; -.22 Emotional vs. rational
  - *Peer ACL*
    - .28 Good natured; .27 Hurried; .28 Masculine
    - .28 Natural; -.37 Dependent; -.30 Emotional
    - -.27 Industrious; -.29 Mild; -.30 Thrifty
    - -.32 Vindictive; -.38 Witty

Scalability

- Males
  - *CPI & other inventory scales*
    - .23 Do; .24 Cs; .21 Sy; .29 Sa; .26 Em; .28 Wb; .30 To
    - .26 Ai; .28 Ie; .19 V3
  - *REP Grid*
    - .25 Masculine vs. feminine; .21 Open vs. closed minded
    - -.27 Closed vs. open minded

(Table continues)

TABLE 6.7: SIGNIFICANT CORRELATES OF SBI MEASURES (CONTINUED)

CONSCIENTIOUSNESS

Scalability

Males

Peer ratings

-.29 Open minded	.26 Conscientiousness consistency	

Peer ACL

-.24 Discreet	-.29 Efficient	
-.23 Individualistic	-.23 Natural	-.24 Persistent
-.29 Progressive	-.28 Serious	-.28 Stingy
-.31 Suggestible	-.24 Thoughtful	-.26 Versatile

Females

CPI & other inventory scales

.23 G P

Self ratings

-.22 Irr elevation

Peer ACL

.27 Confused	.31 Considerate	.32 Emotional
.28 Gentle	.29 Helpful	.28 Kind
.40 Obliging	.32 Sincere	.29 Thoughtful
-.34 Adaptable	-.39 Cruel	-.28 Daring
-.43 Deceitful	-.32 Deliberate	-.29 Forceful
-.29 Masculine		

FRIENDLINESS

Elevation

Males

Target measures

.36 Inventory composite

CPI & other inventory scales

.24 Do	.30 Cs	.31 Sy	.18 Sp	.25 Sa	.33 Em	.24 To
.24 Ac	.24 Ai	.24 Ie	-.29 V1	.21 V3	-.20 S Anx	-.28 B I
.21 G F	.27 G P					

Self ratings/ REP Grid

.21 Con importance	-.20 Attractive vs. unattractive
.29 Independent vs. dependent	

Peer ACL

.24 Effeminate	.25 Intolerant	.22 Mature
.32 Moderate	.25 Queer	.23 Retiring
.29 Stolid	-.22 Fickle	-.27 Honest
-.25 Indifferent	-.25 Informal	-.23 Reckless

(Table continues)

TABLE 6.7: SIGNIFICANT CORRELATES OF SBI MEASURES (CONTINUED)

FRIENDLINESS

Females

Target measures

.53 Inventory composite	.34 Behavior cluster					

CPI & other inventory scales

.42 Do	.41 Cs	.40 Sy	.32 Sp	.34 Sa	.34 In	.46 Em
.33 Re	.31 So	.22 Sc	.43 Gi	.22 Cm	.44 Wb	.40 To
.27 Ac	.35 Ai	.47 Ie	.38 Py	-.25 Fe	-.33 V1	.54 V3
-.26 Pv S-C	-.21 Pb S-C	-.38 S Anx	-.42 Sum S-C	-.36 B I	.24 G G	.27 G F
.35 G P						

Self ratings

-.22 Con elevation	.34 Fre elevation

REP Grid

-.23 Aloof vs. friendly	-.30 Emotional vs. rational
.22 Self-conscious vs. un-self conscious	

Behavior report

-.22 Hours alone	.38 Hours with friends
-.26 Hours studying	.23 Times happy
.27 Times sociable	.25 Times confident

Peer ACL

.35 Dreamy	.34 Hurried	.30 Quick
.31 Self-seeking	-.27 Complaining	-.29 Dissatisfied
-.32 Fearful	-.35 Hard-headed	-.37 Irritable
-.30 Mild	-.33 Obnoxious	-.30 Resentful
-.30 Sulky		

Scalability

Males

CPI & other inventory scales

.26 Cs	.21 Em	.27 Cm	.25 Wb	.26 Ac	.23 Ai	.18 Ie
.19 Fx	.22 V3	.22 Pv S-C				

Self ratings/REP grid

.19 Con elevation	-.29 Con variability	.22 Irr variability
-.26 Attractive vs. unattractive		.23 Number of elicited constructs

Peer ACL

.29 Active	.24 Emotional	.27 Nervous
.23 Reflective	-.23 Complaining	-.22 Disorderly
-.25 Honest	-.26 Indifferent	-.24 Progressive
-.30 Reckless	-.24 Submissive	-.32 Tactless

Females

CPI & other inventory scales

.30 Do	.28 Sy	.27 Sp	.24 Sa	.28 In	.22 Em	.22 Cm
.24 Wb	.22 Ie	-.22 V1	.27 V2	.24 V3	-.21 Pb S-C	
-.29 S Anx	-.34 Sum S-C					

(Table continues)

TABLE 6.7: SIGNIFICANT CORRELATES OF SBI MEASURES (CONTINUED)

FRIENDLINESS

Scalability

Females

REP Grid

-.22 Lazy vs. achieving		-.24 Emotional vs. rational				

Behavior report

-.23 Times bored	-.27 Times embarrassed	

Peer ratings

.29 Achieving

Peer ACL

.36 Good-natured	.36 Hurried	.35 Loyal
-.29 Complaining	-.31 Dissatisfied	-.32 Emotional
-.34 Humorous	-.31 Lazy	-.32 Mild
-.32 Nervous		

IRRITABILITY/CYNICISM[a]

Elevation

Males

Target measures

(none)

CPI & other inventory scales

-.24 Cs	-.20 Sy	-.21 In	-.25 Em	-.23 Gi	-.22 Wb	-.32 Ac
-.27 Ai	-.20 Py	-.19 V3	.26 B I	-.24 G F	-.26 G P	

REP Grid

.24 Attractive vs. unattractive

-.22 Independent vs. dependent

Behavior report

.20 Times bored

Peer ACL

.27 Disorderly	.23 Honest	.27 Indifferent
.25 Informal	.24 Relaxed	-.24 Active
-.24 Effeminate	-.23 Intolerant	-.24 Organized
-.28 Queer	-.28 Retiring	-.25 Unscrupulous

Females

Target measures

(none)

CPI & other inventory scales

-.25 Do	-.27 Cs	-.23 Sy	-.23 In	-.24 Em	-.37 Re	-.38 So
-.50 Gi	-.41 Wb	-.38 To	-.35 Ac	-.24 Ai	-.40 Ie	-.33 Py
-.23 V2	-.46 V3	.25 Pv S-C	.21 Pb S-C	.26 S Anx	.36 Sum S-C	.39 B I
-.28 G F	.24 G P					

Self ratings/REP Grid

-.25 Con elevation	-.24 Con importance	.34 Emotional vs. rational

(Table continues)

Table 6.7: Significant correlates of SBI Measures (continued)

Irritability/cynicism

Elevation

Females

Behavior report

-.22 Hours with friends .23 Times nervous
-.22 Times sociable

Peer ACL

.32 Bitter	.35 Complaining	.43 Dissatisfied
.36 Fearful	.32 Hard-headed	.32 Irritable
.36 Obnoxious	.44 Resentful	.29 Restless
.44 Sulky	.29 Tough	.34 Vindictive
-.32 Civilized	-.28 Foolish	

Scalability

Males

CPI & other inventory scales

.33 Cs	.21 Sy	.23 Sa	.30 Em	.23 So	.29 Gi	.31 Cm
.30 Wb	.19 To	.39 Ac	.24 Ai	.23 Ie	.22 V3	.20 G F

Self ratings

.21 Con elevation -.30 Con variability .19 Con importance
-.20 Fre variability

REP Grid

-.38 Attractive vs. unattractive
.21 Number of elicited constructs

Peer ACL

.23 Poised	-.30 Disorderly	-.24 Forgetful
-.24 Mischievous	-.26 Rebellious	-.24 Reckless
-.31 Rude		

Females

CPI & other inventory scales

.39 Do	.32 Cs	.30 Sy	.26 Sp	.23 Sa	.39 In	.33 Em
.25 Re	.35 So	.26 Cm	.28 Wb	.30 Ac	.22 Ai	.26 Ie
.25 Py	-.22 Fe	-.33 V1	.29 V2	.36 V3	-.22 Pv S-C	
.31 S Anx	.27 G G	-.33 Sum S-C-.23 B I				

Self ratings

-.22 Irr elevation

REP Grid

-.25 Irresponsible vs. conscientious

Peer ratings/ACL

-.31 Dependent (rating)	.38 Good natured	.34 Hurried
.28 Stable	-.31 Dependent	-.30 Emotional
-.29 Thrifty		

(Table continues)

TABLE 6.7: SIGNIFICANT CORRELATES OF SBI MEASURES (CONTINUED)

SELF-CONSCIOUSNESS

Elevation

Males

Target measures

.43 Inventory composite .20 Behavior cluster

CPI & other inventory scales

-.37 Do -.36 Cs -.39 Sy -.47 Sp -.41 Sa -.39 In -.28 Em

.18 So .22 Sc -.20 Ai -.26 Ie -.28 Fx .29 Fe .42 V1

.22 V2 .38 S Anx .30 Sum S-C

Self ratings

-.21 Fre elevation .19 Scn elevation

Behavior report

-.20 Times late for class/appointments

.29 Hours studying .23 Hours in class .19 Times nervous

Peer ACL

.36 Smug -.25 Careless -.23 Complaining

-.29 Curious -.23 Demanding -.29 Dreamy

-.21 Foolish -.25 Forceful -.22 Forgetful

-.26 Generous -.26 Headstrong -.25 Irresponsible

-.40 Jolly -.23 Kind -.24 Peculiar

-.29 Pleasant -.27 Preoccupied -.28 Reckless

-.23 Sarcastic -.30 Sensitive -.25 Spontaneous

-.31 Zany

Females

Target measures

.42 Inventory composite .23 Behavior cluster

CPI & other inventory scales

-.24 Do -.23 Cs -.35 Sy -.44 Sp -.37 Sa -.28 In .32 Re

.35 So .33 Sc -.23 Ie -.25 Py .32 V1 .23 Pb S-C

.29 S Anx .27 Sum S-C

Self ratings

-.24 Fre elevation

REP Grid/Behavior report

-.29 Independent vs. dependent -.22 Serious vs. playful

.22 Times embarrassed

Peer ACL

.31 Bossy .29 Civilized .45 Conservative

.30 Contented .36 Cowardly

.30 Interests narrow .31 Mannerly .36 Meek

.38 Peaceable .32 Prudish .33 Unemotional

.30 Withdrawn -.29 Affected -.28 Clever

-.31 Coarse -.33 Excitable

-.36 Pleasure-seeking -.31 Sexy -.38 Show-off

(Table continues)

TABLE 6.7: SIGNIFICANT CORRELATES OF SBI MEASURES (CONTINUED)

	SELF-CONSCIOUSNESS						
Scalability							
Males							
CPI & other inventory scales							
	.24 Do	.24 Cs	.28 Sy	.35 Sp	.27 Em	.25 Cm	.27 Fx
	-.23 S Anx	-.22 Sum S-C					
Self ratings							
	.20 Fre elevation		-.19 Scn importance				
REP Grid							
	.24 Rational vs. emotional						
Behavior report							
	.21 Hours with friends		-.22 Hours studying				
	-.21 Hours in class		.28 Hours with friends				
	-.24 Times nervous						
Peer ACL							
	.25 Curious		.29 Dreamy		.25 Enthusiastic		
	.24 Generous		.28 Healthy		.22 Helpful		
	.26 Jolly		.33 Kind		.32 Pleasant		
	.24 Preoccupied		.29 Relaxed		.23 Sharp-witted		
	.22 Spontaneous		.25 Tactful		.24 Warm		
	.26 Zany		-.26 Distractible		-.26 Fussy		
	-.25 Queer		-.23 Stingy				
Females							
CPI & other inventory scales							
	.26 Do	.40 Cs	.33 Sy	.43 Sp	.34 Sa	.31 In	.30 Em
	.22 To	.29 Ai	.28 Ie	.32 Py	-.28 V1	.30 V3	
	-.31 S Anx	-.25 Sum S-C					
Self ratings							
	-.23 Con importance		-.26 Fre variability				
Peer ACL							
	.32 Obliging		.29 Unassuming		-.34 Anxious		
	-.28 Civilized		-.32 Cowardly		-.31 Modest		
	-.31 Simple						

Notes: All correlates shown are significant at $p < .05$. Ach= Achievement, Con= Conscientiousness, Fre = Friendliness, Irr= Irritability, Scn= Self-Consciousness. California Psychological Inventory (CPI) scales : Do= Dominance, Cs= Capacity for status, Sy = Sociability, Sp= Social Presence, Sa= Self acceptance, In = Independence, Em= Empathy, Re= Responsibility, So= Socialization, Sc= Self-control, Gi= Good impression, Cm= Communality, Wb= Well being, To= Tolerance, Ac= Achievement via Conformance, Ai = Achievement via Independence, Ie= Intellectual efficiency, Py = Psychological mindedness, Fx= Flexibility, Fe= Femininity, V1= Role, V2= Character, V3= Competence. Self-Consciousness Scale (SCS): Pv S-C= Private self-consciousness, Pb S-C= Public self-consciousness, S anx= Social Anxiety. Guilford Zimmerman Temperament Survey (GZTS) scales: G F= Friendliness, G P= Personal relations, G G= General Activity. Additional measures: B I= Buss-Durkee Hostility Inventory - Irritability.

[a]See text.

Scalability. In males, for the *Achievement scalability* measure, three clusters of significant correlates can be isolated. High scorers are, first, conventional, compliant, and norm-cathecting, possibly to the point of rigidity. Second, they appear to be sociable and oriented towards others, perhaps to the point of shallowness. Third, they are seen as disorganized and casual. In contrast to the picture for the males, the correlates of Achievement scalability in females appear somewhat less focussed, although the central theme appears to be one of passivity and inaction.

Males scoring high in *Conscientiousness scalability* appear inflexible to their peers but capable and tolerant on the CPI. Females appear cautious, sensitive, and kind.

For the remaining traits, the zero-order correlates of scalability were somewhat determined by the overlap between scalability and elevation. *Friendliness scalability*, in the males' self-report data, suggests a theme of caution and hyper-sensitivity to social norms. Among females, this measure was associated with ratings of companionship, adjustment, and activity.

For the intended measure of irritability, better understood as cynicism, the correlates are again largely dependent upon the relation between elevation and scalability ($r = -.58$). In males, *Irritability/cynicism scalability* is associated with caution and poise; in females, high scalability is associated with adjustment to and acceptance of social norms.

In males, *self-consciousness scalability* implies extraversion and "un-self consciousness." In females, no clear set of relations emerges.

6.4.2 Moderated multiple regression analyses

It will be recalled that, for each of the five traits, three composite target variables were constructed against which to examine the utility of scalability as a moderator variable (see Table 6.2). Correlations between the elevation measures and the targets constitute evidence of the validity of the scales. For all but the irritability scale, one or more of the targets was significantly correlated with criteria.

In Table 6.8, moderated multiple regression analyses are presented for all five traits. Prediction equations for each target variable are shown, for each trait, at each of three levels of scalability. An increased slope for the high scalability group indicates greater predictability for this group (Cohen & Cohen, 1975; Stone & Hollenbeck, 1984). This table also shows the Multiple R and R^2 after each of three regression steps (entry of elevation, entry of scalability, entry of product term). (*Text continues on page 99*).

TABLE 6.8: MODERATOR EFFECTS IN THE SBI STUDY

Trait word - sample Step	R	R^2	Linear equations	Scalability level
Achievement- Males				
1	37 *	14	Self report = 26.95 + (.471 X Elev)	*at* t_{scal} = 35
2	37	14	= 31.60 + (.396 X Elev)	*at* t_{scal} = 50
3	37	14	= 36.25 + (.321 X Elev)	*at* t_{scal} = 65
1	14	02	Peer rating = 59.63 - (.145 X Elev)	*at* t_{scal} = 35
2	38 *	14	= 38.93 + (.170 X Elev)	*at* t_{scal} = 50
3	41	17	= 18.23 + (.485 X Elev)	*at* t_{scal} = 65
1	18	03	Behavior log = 61.55- (.200 X Elev)	*at* t_{scal} = 35
2	25	06	= 41.30 + (.160 X Elev)	*at* t_{scal} = 50
3	32 *	10	= 21.05 + (.520 X Elev)	*at* t_{scal} = 65
Achievement- Females				
1	35 *	12	Self report = 51.56 - (.021 X Elev)	*at* t_{scal} = 35
2	36	13	= 33.30 + (.309 X Elev)	*at* t_{scal} = 50
3	41	17	= 15.05 + (.639 X Elev)	*at* t_{scal} = 65
1	11	01	Peer rating = 78.63 - (.595 X Elev)	*at* t_{scal} = 35
2	13	02	= 53.43 - (.130 X Elev)	*at* t_{scal} = 50
3	32 *	10	= 28.23 + (.335 X Elev)	*at* t_{scal} = 65
1	08	01	Behavior log= 51.57- (.070 X Elev)	*at* t_{scal} = 35
2	11	01	= 46.92 + (.050 X Elev)	*at* t_{scal} = 50
3	13	02	= 42.27 + (.170 X Elev)	*at* t_{scal} = 65
Conscientiousness - Males				
1	33 *	11	Self report = 48.89 - (.051 X Elev)	*at* t_{scal} = 35
2	40 *	16	= 31.40 + (.354 X Elev)	*at* t_{scal} = 50
3	47 *	22	= 13.19 + (.759 X Elev)	*at* t_{scal} = 65
1	23 *	05	Peer rating = 55.13 - (.114 X Elev)	*at* t_{scal} = 35
2	25	06	= 38.00 + (.201 X Elev)	*at* t_{scal} = 50
3	29	08	= 20.87 + (.516 X Elev)	*at* t_{scal} = 65
1	21 *	04	Behavior log = 49.65+ (.067 X Elev)	*at* t_{scal} = 35
2	28	08	= 38.93 + (.231 X Elev)	*at* t_{scal} = 50
3	29	08	= 28.20 + (.396 X Elev)	*at* t_{scal} = 65

(Table continues)

TABLE 6.8: MODERATOR EFFECTS IN THE SBI STUDY (CONTINUED)

Trait word - sample Step	R	R^2	Linear equations	Scalability level
Conscientiousness - Females				
1	36 *	13	Self report = 20.45 + (.511 X Elev)	*at* t_{scal} = *35*
2	41 *	17	= 32.45 + (.346 X Elev)	*at* t_{scal} = *50*
3	43	18	= 44.45 + (.181 X Elev)	*at* t_{scal} = *65*
1	12	01	Peer rating = 32.81 + (.267 X Elev)	*at* t_{scal} = *35*
2	33 *	11	= 42.35 + (.177 X Elev)	*at* t_{scal} = *50*
3	34	12	= 51.89 + (.087 X Elev)	*at* t_{scal} = *65*
1	03	00	Behavior log = 46.59 + (.102 X Elev)	*at* t_{scal} = *35*
2	05	00	= 49.40 + (.042 X Elev)	*at* t_{scal} = *50*
3	07	00	= 50.20 - (.018 X Elev)	*at* t_{scal} = *65*
Friendliness - Males				
1	36 *	13	Self report = 27.54 + (.404 X Elev)	*at* t_{scal} = *35*
2	36	13	= 31.14 + (.344 X Elev)	*at* t_{scal} = *50*
3	36	13	= 34.74 + (.284 X Elev)	*at* t_{scal} = *65*
1	03	00	Peer rating = 62.98 - (.287 X Elev)	*at* t_{scal} = *35*
2	05	00	= 44.27 + (.058 X Elev)	*at* t_{scal} = *50*
3	20	04	= 25.57 + (.403 X Elev)	*at* t_{scal} = *65*
1	08	01	Behavior log = 54.89 - (.061 X Elev)	*at* t_{scal} = *35*
2	13	02	= 42.20 + (.149 X Elev)	*at* t_{scal} = *50*
3	20	04	= 29.51 + (.359 X Elev)	*at* t_{scal} = *65*
Friendliness - Females				
1	53 *	28	Self report = 26.26 + (.598 X Elev)	*at* t_{scal} = *35*
2	58 *	34	= 19.39 + (.643 X Elev)	*at* t_{scal} = *50*
3	58	34	= 12.52 + (.688 X Elev)	*at* t_{scal} = *65*
1	17	03	Peer rating = 43.68 + (.112 X Elev)	*at* t_{scal} = *35*
2	20	04	= 46.53 + (.097 X Elev)	*at* t_{scal} = *50*
3	20	04	= 49.38 + (.082 X Elev)	*at* t_{scal} = *65*
1	34 *	12	Behavior log = 25.71 + (.575 X Elev)	*at* t_{scal} = *35*
2	37	14	= 26.16 + (.500 X Elev)	*at* t_{scal} = *50*
3	38	14	= 26.61 + (.425 X Elev)	*at* t_{scal} = *65*

(Table continues)

TABLE 6.8: MODERATOR EFFECTS IN THE SBI STUDY (CONTINUED)

Trait word - sample Step	R	R^2	Linear equations	Scalability level
Irritability/cynicism[a] *- Males*				
1	14	02	Self report = 50.51 + (.024 X Elev)	*at* t_{scal} = *35*
2	16	03	= 45.80 + (.099 X Elev)	*at* t_{scal} = *50*
3	16	03	= 41.09 + (.174 X Elev)	*at* t_{scal} = *65*
1	07	00	Peer rating = 57.67 - (.157 X Elev)	*at* t_{scal} = *35*
2	07	00	= 54.35 - (.097 X Elev)	*at* t_{scal} = *50*
3	08	01	= 51.04 - (.037 X Elev)	*at* t_{scal} = *65*
1	05	00	Behavior log = 28.17 + (.423 X Elev)	*at* t_{scal} = *35*
2	06	00	= 44.82 + (.093 X Elev)	*at* t_{scal} = *50*
3	21 *	04	= 61.47 - (.234 X Elev)	*at* t_{scal} = *65*
Irritability/cynicism - Females				
1	16	03	Self report = 28.47 + (.346 X Elev)	*at* t_{scal} = *35*
2	24	06	= 33.64 + (.316 X Elev)	*at* t_{scal} = *50*
3	24	06	= 38.82 + (.286 X Elev)	*at* t_{scal} = *65*
1	07	00	Peer rating = 48.31 + (.091 X Elev)	*at* t_{scal} = *35*
2	07	00	= 48.64 + (.046 X Elev)	*at* t_{scal} = *50*
3	11	01	= 48.97 + (.001 X Elev)	*at* t_{scal} = *65*
1	13	02	Behavior log = 48.31 + (.091 X Elev)	*at* t_{scal} = *35*
2	17	03	= 48.64 + (.046 X Elev)	*at* t_{scal} = *50*
3	17	03	= 48.97 + (.001 X Elev)	*at* t_{scal} = *65*
Self-Consciousness - Males				
1	43 *	18	Self report = 46.48 + (.098 X Elev)	*at* t_{scal} = *35*
2	43	18	= 29.77 + (.413 X Elev)	*at* t_{scal} = *50*
3	49 *	24	= 13.06 + (.728 X Elev)	*at* t_{scal} = *65*
1	08	01	Peer rating = 52.80 + (.009 X Elev)	*at* t_{scal} = *35*
2	09	01	= 49.77 + (.054 X Elev)	*at* t_{scal} = *50*
3	10	01	= 46.74 + (.099 X Elev)	*at* t_{scal} = *65*
1	20 *	04	Behavior log = 40.52 + (.229 X Elev)	*at* t_{scal} = *35*
2	25	06	= 44.19 + (.109 X Elev)	*at* t_{scal} = *50*
3	27	07	= 47.87 - (.011 X Elev)	*at* t_{scal} = *65*

(Table continues)

TABLE 6.8: MODERATOR EFFECTS IN THE SBI STUDY (CONTINUED)

Trait word - sample Step	R	R^2	Linear equations	Scalability level
Self-Consciousness - Females				
1	42 *	18	Self report = 27.58 + (.517 X Elev)	*at t_{scal} = 35*
2	46	21	= 34.13 + (.337 X Elev)	*at t_{scal} = 50*
3	47	22	= 40.69 + (.157 X Elev)	*at t_{scal} = 65*
1	12	01	Peer rating = 42.85 + (.115 X Elev)	*at t_{scal} = 35*
2	15	02	= 43.36 + (.070 X Elev)	*at t_{scal} = 50*
3	16	03	= 43.87 + (.025 X Elev)	*at t_{scal} = 65*
1	23 *	05	Behavior log = 30.89 + (.406 X Elev)	*at t_{scal} = 35*
2	24	06	= 39.68 + (.226 X Elev)	*at t_{scal} = 50*
3	27	07	= 48.47 + (.046 X Elev)	*at t_{scal} = 65*

Notes: Scal = Scalability, Elev = Elevation.

[a]See text.

*Increment in R^2 significant at $p < .05$.

Because the SBI irritability measure was not valid, the moderator analysis for this trait word is somewhat bizarre, and is included here only for the sake of completeness. This analysis assesses the contributions of cynicism, cynicism scalability, and cynicism scalability as a moderator in the prediction of the irritability targets. Not surprisingly, the measure of scalability for this trait did not contribute to prediction, either directly or indirectly, in the regression analysis. In 18 significance tests for this trait (three targets X two sexes X three regression steps), only one result was statistically significant, this being a reverse moderator effect for males in the prediction of the behavior cluster. Because of the lack of validity for the elevation measure, results for this trait are presented separately in Table 6.9, which summarizes the moderator analyses. Results for the remaining traits are considered in more detail in the following paragraphs.

Direct relations between scalability and target variables. For *Achievement*, in males, reversed scalability contributed significantly to the predictability of the Peer cluster, and showed a similar trend in the Behavior cluster. That is, highly scalable males were seen as less achieving by their peers, and spent less time studying and in class. In this sample of persons, behaviors, and situations, high scalability suggest an orientation towards *Achievement* which is relatively situation bound, and less pervasive in its influence than for the less scalable persons.

TABLE 6.9: SUMMARY OF HIERARCHICAL REGRESSION ANALYSES

Traits averaged over target measures	Elevation R	(R^2)	Scalability R	(R^2)	Interaction R	(R^2)
Achievement						
Males[a]	+.23	(.05)	.39	(.15)	.39	(.15)
Females	+.18	(.03)	.20	(.04)	+.29	(.08)
Conscientiousness						
Males	+.26	(.07)	+.31	(.10)	+.35	(.12)
Females	+.17	(.03)	+.26	(.07)	.28	(.08)
Friendliness						
Males	+.16	(.03)	.18	(.04)	+.25	(.06)
Females	+.35	(.12)	-.39	(.15)	.39	(.15)
Self-Consciousness						
Males	+.24	(.06)	.26	(.07)	.29	(.08)
Females	+.26	(.07)	.29	(.08)	-.31	(.10)
Average (excluding irritability)						
(over sex, trait, target)	.23	(.05)	.28	(.08)	.32	(.10)
Irritability						
Males	.09	(.01)	.10	(.01)	.15	(.02)
Females	.12	(.01)	+.16	(.03)	.17	(.03)
Global average						
(over sex, trait, target)	.21	(.04)	.25	(.06)	.28	(.08)

Note: N = 78 to 115 Males, 54 to 89 Females

[a]Sign of zero order (Elevation) or partial (Scalability, Product) coefficient is shown where average increment in R^2 is .02 or greater.

Similarly, in females, the negative relation between the inventory measure of *Friendliness* and scalability scores for that trait suggests that a sensitivity to situational demands is in fact not what we mean by friendliness. Being friendly only to the extent required by the situation implies at best a lack of spontaneity; at worst, extreme scalability in friendliness would suggest a calculating and cold interpersonal style.

For the trait of *Conscientiousness*, scalability scores showed a significant positive correlation to one or more target variables in both sexes. The interpretation of this is clear: Part of what we mean by conscientiousness is an awareness, or even over-awareness, of situational demands.

Moderator effects. A significant moderator effect was found for one target variable in each sex for *Achievement*; moderator effects were in the predicted direction for five of the six statistical tests for this trait. For this trait, on this sample, scalability leads to greater predictability. Figure 6.3 illustrates one of these results, the non-significant finding for the prediction of the inventory composite in the female sample. Here, the equations from Table 6.8 are solved for several values of elevation and scalability, revealing the pattern of greater predictability for the highly scalable subjects.

For two of the remaining traits, Males showed significant positive moderator effects for the prediction of the inventory measures. For *Conscientiousness*, the other targets showed non- significant trends in the same direction. The results for *Self-Consciousness* were somewhat weaker, with only one of the two other targets showing the same trend as the significant moderator. For *Friendliness*, no significant moderator effect was found.

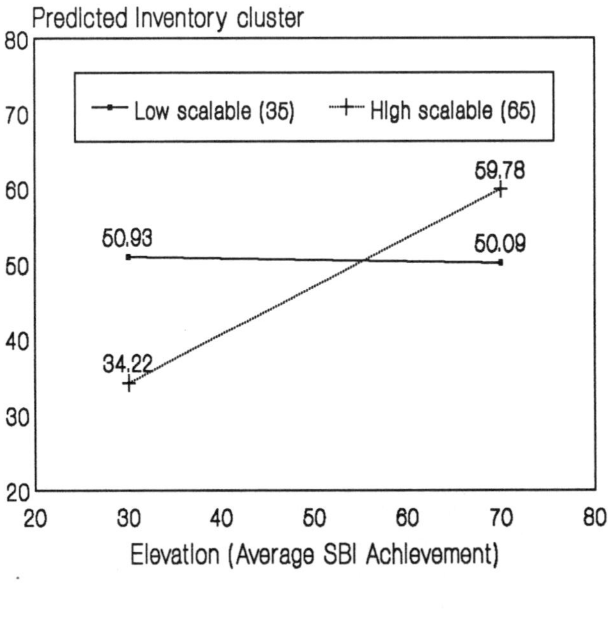

Figure 6.3: Prediction of Achievement inventory composite from SBI Elevation for two different levels of scalability. All variables distributed (50, 10); $N = 89$ Females.

In summary, these analyses indicate that, in both sexes, both scalability and the product term contribute to the prediction of *Achievement* and *Conscientiousness*. Weaker results were found for a main effect of scalability in the prediction of *Friendliness* (in females) and a moderator effect in the prediction of *Self-consciousness* (in males).

Over all traits and measures, eleven of the thirty elevation measures contributed significantly (at $p < .05$); all of these correlations were positive. Scalability and product terms increased the predictability of a number of measures. Five of the tests showed a significant increment following the inclusion of scalability; two of these were positive and three were reversed. Five of the product terms were significant, four in the expected direction. Scalability was an impressive adjunct to the more traditional measures. Even when one includes results for the failed measure of irritability, the average R^2 after elevation alone (.04) is doubled (to .08) following the two steps which make use of the scalability scoring approach.

6.5 Discussion

Scalability measures appear reliable. When scalability is computed on the non-extreme items, the scalability measures are essentially unrelated to elevation for two traits, *Achievement* and *Conscientiousness*. In moderated multiple regression analyses, these same variables showed significant moderator effects.

For the remaining traits, the increment in predictability afforded by the measurement of scalability was more modest. Nonetheless, the overall contribution of scalability in prediction, both as a moderator variable and in direct relations with target variables, leaves room for optimism.

6.5.1 Scalability and reliability

The importance of the moderator findings for the inventory composites might be questioned on the grounds that these measures are of essentially the same data type as the elevation scales.

That is, if SBI elevation and the inventory measures tap essentially the same concept, then one might combine them to form a single self report scale. For example, *Achievement* would be CPI Achievement via independence plus CPI Capacity for status plus GZTS General Activity plus SBI Achievement. Then the correlation between, on the one hand, the two half measures (CPI + GZTS) and, on the other SBI Achievement becomes an index of reliability. Here, the finding of moderator effects is then a finding of differential reliability for different groups. For highly scalable persons, measures of elevation are simply more reliable than for less scalable individuals. Because scalability is defined as simply consistency in responding, the finding of a moderator effect in the prediction of inventory measures would appear to be somewhat tautological.

But, although the significance of a moderator effect is attenuated due to the similarity between the response formats in the SBI and the inventory measures, it is not reduced as much as this argument would claim. First, the relationship between scalability and reliability is considerably more complex than argument would suggest. Second, even if the inventory measures were completely identical in response format to the SBI, the finding of a moderator effect would still suggest that at least the scalability scores were generalizable to a broader set of items from within the same domain. Third, the finding of differential reliability still has implications for validity, because reliability scores impose a ceiling upon validity.

6.5.2 Scalability as norm-sensitivity

A second possible criticism of the findings in this chapter concerns the high correlation between the *Achievement* and *Conscientiousness* measures. The elevation scores for these traits are highly similar. Even though the scalability measures are less intercorrelated than the elevation measures, it can nonetheless be argued that the findings for the *two* measures of really represent an increment in the predictability of only one trait. The only interpretable correlations for these two measures of scalability (for *Achievement* in males and *Conscientiousness* in females) suggest the same *norm-sensitivity* that described the highly scalable subjects in the study of scalability in hostility (Chapter 4). In the naturalistic measurement approach embodied by the SBI, the *general* component of scalability scores is probably sufficient to account for all of the correlates of scalability in *Achievement* and *Conscientiousness*. In the remaining traits, significant correlates appear to reflect a blend of general scalability with the specific content of that trait (e.g., *Friendliness* scalability measures norm-sensitivity and friendliness).

The lack of unique correlates of scalability measures may be because *specific scalability* is not important or implicative in personality research. More likely, the present set of validational measures lacked the depth required to capture the subtle differences among the different measures of scalability. What is needed is a study which combines the assessment method of Chapter 4 with the larger sample of the present study. Such an undertaking is, unfortunately, beyond the scope of the present work.

A less ambitious investigation, however, will provide some additional information concerning some different possible interpretations of scalability scores. The SBI measures of scalability are not independent (all rely on the same set of items); consequently, relations among different measures of scalability are confounded by mathematical necessity, and do not reflect simple conceptual overlap. In the next chapter, measures of scalability will be computed on two traditional personality inventories, the CPI and the Multidimensional Personality Questionnaire (MPQ; Tellegen, 1982). This will allow both an examination of unconfounded relations among scalability measures, and an investigation into the utility of extending the scalability approach to the scoring of traditional measures.

7

Scalability on Standard Personality Inventories

Scalability is an entirely general measurement approach. Measures of residuals can be computed on any rectangular matrix; where this is a person X item matrix with entries describing elevation, these residuals, once reversed, provide a measure of scalability.

The matrix of responses of a sample of persons to a set of fixed-choice questionnaire items, such as a traditional personality inventory, fulfills these requirements. Scalability scores computed on such a matrix are particularly likely to be informative where the response format provides for more than two options. (In the dichotomous case, intra-individual variability scores are completely determined by elevation scores; because scalability scores are mathematically similar to simple variabilities, a high degree of entailment can be anticipated).

Because scalability can be readily scored on responses to standard personality tests, it is worthwhile to examine whether or not individual differences in scalability over the items of standard personality inventories can contribute to the prediction of non-test criteria: Scalability effects, if robust, would be a "free lunch" in that increased predictability could be obtained without additional data.

In the present chapter, I investigate the properties of scalability on two personality inventories, the CPI and the Multidimensional Personality Questionnaire (MPQ; Tellegen, 1982). This investigation will also permit examination of some additional questions concerning the utility and significance of scalability scores. Accordingly, prior to my empiricism, I will consider four separate interpretations of individual differences in consistency, and outline some possible distinctions between these. I then propose that it is useful to "break down" a sample-wide moderator effect into individual scores, and thereby more closely examine the improvement (or decrement) in prediction that occurs when a moderator is introduced. Following this, I will examine the potential moderating role of consistency, as indexed by scalability, on the two inventories.

7.1 Four interpretations of individual differences in consistency

It has been argued that scalability is an approach to measuring "consistency." But, as was seen in Chapter 2, the concept of consistency is broad. Indeed, individual differences in consistency may be interpreted in at least four separate ways. The first three interpretations of consistency may be described as deriving from personality metatheory, personality research, and applied psychology, respectively. At a different level of analysis, a fourth interpretation of consistency stems from psychometric concerns. Although three of these perspectives have been discussed in previous chapters, I will review all four positions in the following paragraphs.

7.1.1 Consistency in personality metatheory: Trait relevance

As the reader will recall from Chapter 1, two major ontological conceptions of personality may be distinguished. For Allport (1937), these were the "biosocial" and the "biophysical" positions. I have suggested that the labels *constructive* and *structural* are more descriptive: According to the first of these positions, personality traits are best understood as social constructions, according to the second, traits are considered to be veritable psychological structures. For reasons described previously, both positions are in essence sound, yet both are incomplete. That is, the constructive or biosocial position is correct insofar as all words attain meaning only through social discourse, but this conception of traits as social labels does not invalidate the notion that there are structural entities - or personal dispositions - to which trait labels can properly be ascribed. For its part, the structural or biophysical position cannot stand alone, for a truly "personal" disposition would of necessity remain preverbal, incommunicable, and therefore unintelligible (Wittgenstein, 1953).

The biosocial and biophysical positions may be reconciled by viewing personality assessment as a mapping process. In this process, measures of consistency may be interpreted as indices of the correspondence between trait words and personal dispositions, or, equivalently, of the "relevance" of traits for individuals. Recently, a similar interpretation of consistency as trait relevance has been put forward by Baumeister and Tice (1988).

7.1.2 Consistency in personality research: Global sensitivity to norms

Apparent consistency with respect to a trait may not be due to the appropriateness of a specific trait word in characterizing a person, but, rather, to a global consistency on the part of that person. In Chapter 2, a series of studies of global consistency was examined, including papers by Allport and Vernon (1933), Block, (1961), Campus (1974), Cattell, (1943), Fiske, (1957), Glaser (1952), Goldberg (1978) and Holden, Helmes, Fekken, and Jackson (1985). In these papers, there was little consensus concerning the empirical implications of global consistency. Several possible sources for this lack of consensus were considered, including (1) the argument that global consistency is confounded with stylistic variance, which itself is confounded with measures of many substantive personality traits (Goldberg, 1978; Jackson, 1986), (2) the idea that global measures of consistency may simply be too heterogeneous to be meaningful, and (3) the possibility that global consistency may be related only indirectly (i.e., as a moderator) to other measures of personality).

7.1.3 Consistency in applied psychology: Protocol validity

Under a third interpretation, consistency *per se* is not the focus of interest. The absence of consistency, however, is considered implicative: Inconsistency is attributed to an inability to comprehend items or instructions or to a lack of motivation on the part of the test-taker. Inconsistency appears as inattentive or random responding, and inconsistent protocols should be considered "invalid." On several personality inventories, including the MPQ and the Edwards Personal Preference Survey (EPPS; Edwards, 1957), measures of "consistency" are explicitly proposed as validity scales.

7.1.4 Consistency in psychometric theory: Individual differences in generalizability

In Chapter 3, I considered a psychometric rationale for assessing individual differences in consistency. This rationale is not concerned with why individuals might or might not appear "consistent," but simply describes a mechanism through which multi-item measures of individual differences in consistency might be expected to moderate the prediction of external target measures. It was argued that to the extent that test items are representative of the broader universe of "items" (including non-test situations) to which one seeks to generalize, then consistency within the set of test items will imply "consistency" or convergence between these items and non-test measures. A moderator effect is also anticipated by the description of individual differences in consistency as differences in reliability (Fiske & Rice, 1955; Goldberg, 1978; Holden et al., 1985): To the extent that persons differ in their reliability, relations with other measures will be differentially attenuated, and persons will differ in their predictability.

7.2 Distinguishing between different interpretations of consistency

The description of consistency as *generalizability* addresses a different level of analysis than the remaining interpretations, and, as such, remains compatible with each of the alternative positions. The remaining interpretations, however, do make different predictions under certain circumstances.

7.2.1 Correlations among measures of consistency

Of the three substantive interpretations of consistency, *trait relevance* is readily distinguishable from the *global norm-sensitivity* and as *protocol validity* positions. If a measure of consistency for a particular trait measures only the relevance of that trait for that person, then the average correlation among measures of consistency for different traits will be near zero. (For example, the extent to which the trait of "friendliness" is relevant should have no bearing on relevance for "conscientiousness"). Under the remaining interpretations of consistency, measures of consistency for different traits are predicted to be positively related, for each measure of consistency would tap the same latent variable (i.e., global norm-sensitivity or protocol validity).

The interpretations of consistency as *global norm-sensitivity* and as *protocol validity* are similar in several respects. In particular, both predict that measures of consistency for different traits will be related. A distinction can, however, be drawn between these two approaches in that they make different predictions regarding the individuals who will show the greatest benefit when moderator effects are present. This notion of differential moderator effects requires a brief digression.

7.2.2 Individual differences in moderator effects

When an additional variable is included in a regression analysis, the increment in R^2 describes a sample-wide average reduction in squared errors of estimate. Traditionally, moderator effects have been examined on the basis of this summary index alone. But it is possible to break down an R^2 increment at the individual level, and then to examine individual differences in this score, which describes the reduction in squared errors (*RSE*) on an individual basis.

The reduction in squared errors of estimate can be computed by simply computing the difference between (a) the squared error of estimate prior to including the moderator $(Y-\hat{Y}_1)^2$ and (b) the squared error of estimate after including the moderator $(Y-\hat{Y}_2)$. For standardized variables, these errors are directly related to correlations by the equation $1-R^2 = \Sigma (Y-\hat{Y})^2/N$. Because of this, across a sample of individuals, the average *RSE* will be equal to the R^2 increment.

In the present analysis, each of the interpretations of consistency predicts, across persons, a positive moderator effect. To the extent that such a moderator effect is present, when consistency is included in the regression equation, predicted scores will become more extreme for "consistent" persons. Similarly, inclusion of consistency will result in regressed scores for "inconsistent" persons. The moderator effect of consistency could operate by providing increased accuracy for consistent persons, for inconsistent persons, or both of these.

Returning to the question of how to disentangle the interpretations of global norm-sensitivity and protocol validity, it appears that, if consistency is best interpreted as protocol validity, consistency will contribute to predictability for "inconsistent" rather than for "consistent" individuals. That is, the regression equation leads to regressed, more moderate predictions for inconsistent respondents, and these respondents will show a disproportionate amount of beneficial moderator effects, and a higher average RSE. By contrast, under the generalized norm sensitivity position, no specific predictions are made concerning which individuals will benefit from moderator effects. This latter position would be supported if the average RSE is equivalent for "consistent" and for "inconsistent" persons.

In summary, the three substantive interpretations of consistency may be distinguished by examining (a) the correlations among different measures of consistency and (b) individual differences in moderator effects, as assessed by *RSE*. A summary of the distinguishing features of these positions is presented in Table 7.1.

In the analyses to follow, I examine some properties of scalability measures on standard personality inventories. Paralleling the analyses in prior chapters, I begin by describing the construction of a set of target measures, and examining the reliabilities of the scalability measures and their independence from the more elevation measures. I will then examine the role of scalability as a moderator in the prediction of the targets. Finally, I will undertake a series of analyses to explore and test between the different substantive interpretations of consistency.

TABLE 7.1: DISTINGUISHING BETWEEN SUBSTANTIVE INTERPRETATIONS OF CONSISTENCY

Description	Key prediction(s)
Trait relevance	The average correlation among measures of consistency for different traits will be zero.
Global norm-sensitivity	The average correlation among measures of consistency for different traits will be greater than zero. The effect of including consistency in prediction will be no different for "inconsistent" and "consistent" persons, and the average *RSE* for these two groups will therefore be equivalent.
Protocol validity	The average correlation among measures of consistency for different traits will be greater than zero. Including consistency in prediction will have a larger effect for "inconsistent" than for "consistent" persons, and the average *RSE* for these two groups will therefore be greater for inconsistent than for consistent persons.

Note: *RSE* = Reduction in squared error of estimate.

7.3 Method

Subjects were undergraduate students at two universities, the University of California (the *Berkeley* sample) and Oregon State University (the *Corvallis* sample). Each sample was administered one of two personality inventories as well as an autobiographical questionnaire.

The Berkeley sample, consisting of 227 individuals (102 males and 125 females), was administered the MPQ and the autobiographical questionnaire. In the Corvallis sample, 233 individuals (90 males, 143 females) responded to the CPI. Of these persons, 211 (81 males, 143 females) also responded to the autobiographical questionnaire. An additional 101 subjects responded only to the autobiographical questionnaire.

Participants in both the Berkeley and Corvallis samples received both personality feedback (i.e., interpreted scores on the inventories) and experimental credit for undergraduate psychology courses in exchange for their participation. Note that, because several subjects did not complete all measures, the *N* used in particular analyses vary.

7.3.1 Materials and procedure

Personality inventories. The MPQ was administered by Dr. John Kamp of the Institute of Personality Assessment and Research; I am grateful to him for allowing me to use these data. The scales of the MPQ include Well Being, Stress Reaction, Social Potency, Achievement, Social Closeness, Alienation, Aggression, Control, Harmavoidance, Traditionalism, and Absorption. Because the scales of the MPQ are non-overlapping, measures of scalability computed on them will be independent, and will prove suitable for examination of the interrelations among different measures of scalability. Unlike the MPQ, the CPI scales are overlapping, and so are less suitable for examining the question of general *versus* specific scalability. However, the CPI data will be useful for assessing other properties of scalability scores, such as reliability and entailment, as well as for moderated multiple regression analyses.

Both the MPQ and the CPI were administered in a five-choice format. On the MPQ, the standard true-false dichotomy was replaced by responses labelled (a) Definitely true, (b) Somewhat true, (c) Can't really say true or false, (d) Somewhat false, and (e) Definitely false. Approximately half of the Berkeley sample was administered the MPQ via minicomputer; the remainder of this sample was administered a paper-and-pencil version of the inventory. On the CPI, the agree-disagree dichotomy was expanded to (a) Agree strongly, (b) Agree somewhat, (c) Neither agree nor disagree, (d) Disagree somewhat, and (e) Disagree strongly. The CPI was administered via paper and pencil.

Autobiographical data. A set of 150 autobiographical items was administered to the Berkeley sample; a slightly modified subset of 100 of these was administered to the Corvallis students. In the analyses that follow, only the 100 overlapping biographical items are included. These autobiographical items, though similar in form to those of the personality inventories, typically refer to quasi-factual historical events rather than statements of opinion, value, or interest. Sample items include "During the past 12 months, how many days of school or work have you missed because of nervousness or emotional distress?" and "During the past 12 months, how many moving traffic violations have you received?"

On rational grounds, the autobiographical items was reduced to 23 clusters of between two and seven items. On the basis of correlations among these clusters, they were then further reduced to provide ten non-overlapping autobiographical scales. For nine of these autobiographical scales, corresponding inventory measures were readily identified. A description of these scales and their inventory correlates is provided in Table 7.2. A tenth autobiographical scale consisted of items measuring age, frequency of interaction with family and high school friends, and independent living.

Although this scale was reasonably coherent (alpha for 9 items = .66), it was largely uncorrelated with the inventory scales. The closest CPI scale was Femininity/Masculinity, with a correlation of .22; the closest MPQ scale was Social closeness, with a correlation of .14.

TABLE 7.2: AUTOBIOGRAPHICAL CLUSTERS

Cluster name (Number of items, alpha)	Description of content (Corresponding inventory scales, correlations)
Breadth of interests (11, .73)	Hobbies, cultural activities, outdoor activities. *CPI Psychological mindedness, .40* *MPQ Absorption, .28*
Leadership (6, .60)	Public speaking, extraverted achievement. *CPI Dominance, .50* *MPQ Social potency, .56*
Neuroticism (6, .53)	Withdrawal, physical illness, nervousness *CPI Well being, -.51* *MPQ Stress reaction, .49*
Masculinity (5, .64)	Hunting, motorcycle riding *versus* emotionality, crying. *CPI Femininity/Masculinity, -.63* *MPQ Harmavoidance, -.25*
Aggression (9, .62)	Hostility, school misconduct, trouble with authorities. *CPI Socialization, -.49* *MPQ Aggression, .44*
Sociability (5, .57)	Dating, time spent with friends *CPI Sociability, .35* *MPQ Social closeness, .47*
Substance use (4, .57)	Use of alcohol and marijuana versus attendance of regular religious services *CPI Social presence, .35* *MPQ Traditionalism, -.36*
Impulsivity (14, .63)	Missing class, dropping out of school, spontaneity, sensation seeking. *CPI Self control, -.34* *MPQ Control, -.33*
School achievement (8, .76)	Hours of schoolwork, high school GPA, college GPA. *CPI Achievement via Conformance, .32* *MPQ Achievement, .40*

Note: CPI = California Psychological Inventory. (*N* = 204-211) MPQ = Multidimensional Personality Questionnaire. (*N* = 225-227).

Computation of basic scores. For each of the standard CPI and MPQ scales, elevation scores were computed by simply summing items in the keyed direction. Measures of scalability were computed by constructing separate matrices for each of the CPI and MPQ scales and summing, row-wise, the absolute value of the elements of the corresponding double-centered matrices, as described in Chapter 3.

7.4 Results

Table 7.3 describes the reliabilities of the elevation and scalability measures, as well as the linear and non-linear relations between elevation and scalability.

Coefficient alpha reliabilities of the 23 CPI elevation measures ranged from .53 to .86. For the MPQ, the 11 elevation measures had reliabilities ranging from .84 to .93. Reliability estimates of corresponding scalability measures computed on these individual scales were slightly lower, ranging from .58 to .79 for the CPI and .64 to .86 for the MPQ. Across the two inventories, the picture is similar to that of previous chapters: The measures of scalability appeared internally consistent (average alpha = .71), although slightly less so than the measures of elevation (average alpha = .80).

Linear and quadratic entailment of scalability scores by elevation was moderately high, with squared multiple correlations ranging from .00 to .47 on the CPI and .10 to .46 on the MPQ. Linear relations between elevation and scalability on the two inventories were comparable: On the CPI the average R^2_{ES} was .13, on the MPQ, the corresponding value was .15. The inventories differed, however, in that quadratic relations between elevation and scalability were trivial on the CPI, but important on the MPQ. That is, the quadratic contribution to $R^2_{E\text{-}S,S2}$ was only .01 for the CPI, but was .11 for the MPQ. The sign of the quadratic terms was positive for 21 of the 23 CPI scales and for all 11 MPQ scales, indicating increased scalability for persons with extreme elevation scores. As with the SBI, the more reliable measures of scalability generally showed stronger entailment. The correlation between the second and fourth columns of Table 7.3, describing the reliability of scalability scores and entailment, was .57 over the 34 CPI and MPQ scales.

7.4.1 Moderated multiple regression analyses

For each of the autobiographical clusters shown in Table 7.2, regression analyses were undertaken to predict cluster scores from corresponding scales on the CPI (Corvallis sample), and the MPQ (Berkeley sample).

TABLE 7.3 ELEVATION AND SCALABILITY: RELIABILITY AND ENTAILMENT

Scale	Reliability (Coefficient alpha)		Entailment[a]	
	Elevation(E)	Scalability(s)	$R^2_{E\text{-}S}$	$R^2_{E\text{-}S,S^2}$
California Psychological Inventory (CPI)				
Dominance	.83	.75	.04	.05
Capacity for status	.67	.63	.05	.08
Sociability	.79	.70	.30	.30
Social presence	.74	.76	.19	.19
Self acceptance	.62	.66	.18	.18
Independence	.75	.65	.02	-.02
Empathy	.59	.69	.04	.04
Responsibility	.71	.68	.13	-.13
Socialization	.77	.70	.16	.16
Self control	.83	.75	-.03	.05
Good impression	.79	.78	-.15	.15
Communality	.76	.75	.39	.43
Well being	.86	.79	*.46*	.47
Tolerance	.71	.68	.12	.12
Achievement via conformance	.75	.73	.23	.23
Achievement via independence	.75	.73	.10	.10
Intellectual efficiency	.77	.75	.18	.18
Psychological mindedness	.61	.63	.01	.01
Flexibility	.53	.60	.00	.00
Femininity	.68	.58	.02	.03
V1 (Role)	.84	.78	-.06	.11
V2 (Externality)	.74	.70	.07	.08
V3 (Realization)	.86	.74	.14	.15
Average CPI[b]	*.75*	*.71*	*.13*	*.14*
Multidimensional Personality Questionnaire (MPQ)				
Wellbeing	.93	.86	.44	.46
Social potency	.90	.69	.06	.11
Achievement	.87	.71	.08	.17
Social closeness	.89	.69	.29	.36
Stress reaction	.93	.76	.04	.27
Alienation	.90	.79	-.21	.26
Aggression	.87	.72	-.25	.40
Control	.87	.64	.09	.12
Harmavoidance	.88	.71	.00	*.36*
Traditionalism	.84	.68	.05	.10
Absorption	.90	.80	.17	.21
Average MPQ[b]	*.89*	*.73*	*.15*	*.26*

Note: *N* is 445 (total sample) = 228 (CPI) + 227 (MPQ)

[a]Signs refer to zero-order or partial correlations. The largest linear and quadratic effects are italicized. [b]Averages of reliabilities are based on Fisher transformed values.

TABLE 7.4: PREDICTION OF AUTOBIOGRAPHICAL TARGETS - MODERATOR EFFECTS FOR SCALABILITY

Target	*t* (elevation X scalability)[a]		Comb. z[d]	Effect size[e]
	From CPI[b]	From MPQ[c]		
School achievement	2.66*	1.58	3.00*	.14
Sociability	1.16	.88	1.44	.07
Breadth of interests	.92	1.09	1.42	.07
Leadership	.37	.93	.92	.04
Aggression	.77	.32	.77	.04
Substance use	.04	.18	.16	.01
Stereotyp. masculinity	.39	-.66	-.19	-.01
Impulsivity	.81	-1.24	-.30	-.01
Neuroticism	-2.48*	.66	-1.29	-.06

Note: N = 430 - 437.

[a] Values of t for the increase in variance accounted for by the elevation X scalability term in predicting the autobiographical cluster from the corresponding inventory scale. The signs of t values have been reversed, where necessary, so that a positive sign always implies greater predictability for persons higher in scalability. [b]df = 200-207. [c]df = 221-223. [d] $(z\text{CPI} + z\text{MPQ})/2^{1/2}$. [e] $r = z/N^{1/2}$

$^{*}p < .05$

The principal results of the moderated multiple regression analysis are presented in Table 7.4. This table includes t-values for the moderator effect in the prediction of the autobiographical clusters from the CPI (second column) and the MPQ (third column). In order to obtain a more powerful test of the moderator hypothesis and a more stable estimate of the magnitude of its effect, combined z scores were computed following the Stouffer method for each of the targets. Following Zuckerman et al. (1988), estimates of effect size (r) were then obtained by dividing the Stouffer z by the square root of the N for the combined Berkeley and Corvallis samples (Rosenthal, 1978). The statistics for the combined sample are provided in the fourth and fifth columns of the table. For both samples, the largest effect is for the trait of school achievement.

In passing, it should be noted that I also explored an eight-step regression sequence, in which I included the seven steps proposed by Zuckerman et al. (1988) and, in addition, a quadratic elevation term to control for possible confounds between consistency and item extremity. This analysis yielded stronger results: Statistically significant moderating effects of consistency were found for the traits of aggression and sociability in addition to school achievement. The stronger results for this analysis may be attributable to a suppressor effect of the quadratic elevation term, indicating that the component of scalability which is independent of extremity is particularly important in prediction. But given the inherent instability of the repeatedly partialed correlations examined in this approach, and the prior failures to find moderator effects for measures of aggression (Paunonen & Jackson, 1985) and sociability (Chaplin & Goldberg, 1984; Paunonen & Jackson, 1985), a more conservative interpretation of these results seems appropriate.

7.4.2 Analyses to explore different interpretations of consistency

Correlations among measures of scalability. As can be seen in Table 7.5, the measures of scalability on the MPQ were highly related. Of the 55 correlations among the 11 independent measures of scalability, 54 are positive. When the eigenstructure of this matrix is examined, a single unrotated component accounts for 33% of the variance in the MPQ scalability measures, with individual MPQ scales showing loadings ranging from .45 to .71

Although the scales of the CPI are logically linked due to item overlap, it is nonetheless instructive to examine the correlation matrix of scalability measures computed on the CPI scales. Here, all 190 correlations among the 20 scalability measures are positive, with a single unrotated principal component accounting for 54% of the variance in the CPI scalability measures.

TABLE 7.5 - CORRELATIONS AMONG 11 MPQ SCALABILITY MEASURES

	SP	AC	SC	SR	AL	AG	CN	HA	TR	AB
Well being	.24	.28	.31	-.08	.18	.18	.21	.14	.26	.20
Social potency	.32	.20	.28	.19	.14	.22	.05	.18	.29	
Achievement	.26	.11	.18	.20	.37	.16	.23	.25		
Social closeness	.16	.11	.25	.35	.21	.28	.19			
Stress reaction	.14	.03	.21	.13	.25	.25				
Alienation	.31	.23	.22	.15	.17					
Aggression	.28	.24	.23	.14						
Control	.25	.38	.23							
Harmavoidance	.26	.18								
Traditionalism	.28									
Absorption										

Note: N = 225.

Much of the variance in each of the measures of trait-specific scalability is shared, suggesting that on personality inventories, different measures of scalability largely tap the same underlying construct. The predominance of this single component gives credence to the global norm-sensitivity and protocol validity interpretations of scalability.

MPQ factors and scalability. The eleven elevation scales of the MPQ give rise to three higher order factors: Positive Affectivity, Negative Affectivity, and Constraint (Tellegen, 1982). It is interesting to observe the factor structure that underlies the matrix which combines the 22 elevation and scalability scores for the 11 scales. In males, the first rotated factor is a scalability factor: Nine of the eleven scalability measures had their highest loadings on this factor, all of the scalability measures had loadings of at least .35, and none of the elevation measures had loadings greater than .15. The third factor corresponded closely to Tellegen's Negative Affectivity factor; the second factor resembled Positive Affectivity, except that Achievement (which loads on Tellegen's PA factor) here split off and defined its own factor. No factor resembling Control was found in several rotations of the matrix.

In females, the results were quite different. Three factors quite similar to those specified by Tellegen were obtained. With few exceptions, scalability measures loaded on the same variables as the corresponding elevation measures. Factor loadings for scalability measures were higher than those of elevation measures for the Control factor. For the remaining two factors, loadings for scalability measures were, in general, lower than those of corresponding elevation measures. The major result of including the scalability measures was to increase the relative importance of the Control factor, which emerged prior to the Positive and Negative Affectivity factors.

When the sexes are combined, a scalability factor emerges first, followed by the three Tellegen factors. These rotated factors accounted for 38, 29, 20, and 12 percent of the common variance, respectively. Factor loadings are shown in Table 7.6. In these analyses, the relative importance of the scalability factor is inflated due to the inclusion of 11 different scalability measures. Nonetheless, the presence of an independent scalability factor suggests that this measurement approach contributes information which is not present in the regular elevation scores. The psychological significance of this information is, of course, an entirely separate issue.

Individual differences in moderator effects. The only important moderator obtained in the combined sample was for the trait of school achievement. In order to discern which subjects were benefitting from the moderator, I computed individual scores describing the reduction in squared errors of estimate (*RSE*).

TABLE 7.6: ROTATED FACTOR LOADINGS - MPQ ELEVATION AND SCALABILITY

		Factors		
	Scalability	PA	NA	CS
Elevation measures				
Well being	.12	*.94*	-.22	.02
Social potency	-.01	*.54*	.22	-.32
Achievement	-.07	*.31*	.06	.06
Social closeness	-.03	*.45*	-.14	-.03
Stress reaction	-.01	-.45	*.53*	.04
Alienation	-.07	-.26	*.77*	.14
Aggression	-.01	-.11	*.61*	-.16
Control	-.09	-.05	-.06	*.45*
Harmavoidance	-.06	-.06	-.09	*.50*
Traditionalism	-.03	.15	.09	*.55*
Absorption	-.09	.16	*.31*	-.17
Scalability measures				
Well being	.33	*-.59*	.21	-.07
Social potency	*.51*	-.22	-.03	.19
Achievement	*.50*	-.16	-.01	-.13
Social closeness	*.44*	-.11	.16	-.13
Stress reaction	*.45*	.24	-.20	.04
Alienation	*.39*	.07	.37	.08
Aggression	.36	-.01	*.54*	-.10
Control	*.57*	.06	.08	-.37
Harmavoidance	*.35*	.07	.14	-.21
Traditionalism	*.49*	-.03	.04	-.37
Absorption	*.57*	-.14	-.23	.11

Note: N = 225. PA = Positive Affectivity, NA = Negative Affectivity, CS = Control. Highest values in each row are italicized.

According to my arguments in the introduction to this chapter, the *protocol validity* interpretation of consistency will be supported if and only if scalability contributes to predictability for "inconsistent" rather than for "consistent" individuals. But careful consideration reveals that this argument is something of a straw man, for the *RSE* score *cannot* in fact be linearly related to scalability. That is, because each component of the score is orthogonal to scalability, so too is any linear combination of these errors, including the difference between errors on consecutive steps. And empirically, "inconsistents" (persons with negative standard scores on scalability) did not differ from "consistents" (persons with positive standard scores on scalability) in their average *RSE*, with means of .03 and .04, respectively. The correlation between scalability and *RSE* was -.05 for CPI Achievement via Conformance and .03 for MPQ Achievement. Quadratic relations between scalability and

RSE were also largely absent. Instead, scatterplots relating scalability to *RSE* were butterfly-shaped: Persons with extreme scalability scores showed the greatest change upon including scalability in prediction, but these changes were almost as likely to be in the direction of predictive decrements as increments.

The absence of linear and quadratic relations between *RSE* and scalability should not be taken to imply that people do not differ in the *RSE* term. A closer examination of individual differences in *RSE* revealed an important relation between it and the three-way interaction of scalability, predictor and target scores. In essence, much of the sample-wide increment in predictability may be attributed to regressed predictions for low scalability persons in the "off quadrants," i.e., those persons for whom predictor and target were initially divergent. Across the two instruments, the average *RSE* was .22 for the 80 persons who were both low in scalability and for whom predictor and target were initially divergent. This is shown in the upper left quadrant of Table 7.7.

An examination of Table 7.7 reveals that the sample-wide statistics also benefitted from more extreme predictions in the high scalability, on-quadrant group. Here, a relatively large number of persons (155) showed a more modest average improvement in prediction, with an average *RSE* of .06.

TABLE 7.7 : INDIVIDUAL DIFFERENCES IN MODERATOR EFFECTS

	Scalability	
	Low	High
Predictor and target dissimilar		
Low predictor - High target	.20	-.14
High predictor - Low target	.26	-.05
Off - quadrant average[a]	.22	*-.08*
Predictor and target similar		
High predictor - High target	-.13	.04
Low predictor - Low target	-.07	.08
On - quadrant average[b]	*-.09*	*.06*

Note. Entries are the reduction in squared error scores (*RSE*), averaged over the MPQ (N = 225) and CPI (N = 221) data sets. All high and low groups are defined by dividing standardized variables at the origin. Target = School achievement cluster. Predictor = Inventory scale (CPI Achievement via Conformance or MPQ Achievement).

[a]N = 80 (low scalability), 76 (high scalability). [b]N = 125 (low scalability), 155 (high scalability).

Importantly, including moderator effects resulted in a *drop* in predictive accuracy in the remaining cells, with these 201 subjects showing greater squared errors, by an average of .09. These relations are also shown in Table 7.7.

The absence of linear, negative correlations between scalability and *RSE* indicates that measures of scalability are not best interpreted as *a priori* screening devices in prediction. This contradicts a protocol validity interpretation of scalability, and provides indirect support for the remaining interpretation of scalability as generalized norm-sensitivity.

7.5 Discussion

Moderator effects. For measures of conscientiousness, a number of investigators have now found moderator effects for multi-item measures of consistency (see Chapter 6, also Bem & Allen, 1974; Chaplin & Locklear, 1988; Mischel & Peake, 1982). The school achievement target measure, which included items which gauge hours of schoolwork, school attendance, and study habits, lies clearly within this domain, and these findings therefore replicate the results of these earlier studies.

From the standpoint of sample-wide predictability, the present moderator effects are small. However, as the analysis of individual differences showed, individuals differ in the degree to which they benefit from moderator effects. When a moderator is included in prediction, persons with extreme standard scores on the moderator will *necessarily* show the greatest change in predicted scores. Consequently, the effect of including a moderator will differ within the sample, and a weak sample-wide effect may obscure important improvements in prediction for individual persons.

7.5.1 The interpretation of scalability on personality inventories

Different measures of scalability were highly correlated, suggesting that these were best interpreted as largely interchangeable measures of global consistency. In an examination of individual differences in moderator effects, inconsistent persons typically derived no more benefit from the inclusion of scalability than did consistent persons. These analyses give credence to the interpretation of scalability as global norm-sensitivity, and counter-indicate the trait relevance interpretation of scalability, at least on these inventories.

Three reasons for the failure of the "trait relevance" interpretation may be considered. The first of these is that trait relevance is simply superfluous (Burke, Kraut, & Dworkin, 1984). The second is that other methods, such as direct self-ratings, may provide the most sound measures of trait relevance (Zuckerman et al., 1988). The third possibility is that the items, response formats, and/or scales of current personality inventories are ill-suited for the assessment of individual differences in scalability.

Regarding the last of these possibilities, the reader will recall from the previous chapter that there is a tension between *scaling* and *classical* approaches to test construction. Scaling approaches to test construction are most valid when items differ greatly in evocativeness or difficulty. Classical approaches, however, typically have the greatest validity when item difficulties are clustered near the midpoint of the response scale. In addition, where item analysis is used to purify scales, items will be retained on the basis of part-whole correlations; as correlations are sensitive to differences in item distributions, scales will tend to consist of items of similar difficulty (Nunnally, 1978). As a result, item difficulties on standard personality inventories will typically be tightly distributed, and these will provide a less than ideal medium for investigating individual differences in scalability.

The five choice Likert response format examined in the present study, although an improvement over dichotomous formats, may still result in ceiling effects which limit the potential contribution of consistency in prediction (Paunonen & Jackson, 1985). In the study described in Chapter 6, a situation X behavior inventory (the SBI) was used. This more naturalistic format may result in a reduction of ceiling effects.

7.6 Summary

In an examination of individual differences in scalability on two personality inventories, competing interpretations of consistency were disentangled by examining correlations among measures of consistency for different traits and, importantly, individual differences in the reduction of squared error scores afforded by inclusion of the moderator term. These analyses suggest that, on the CPI and the MPQ, measures of scalability are largely interchangeable measures of global norm-sensitivity. On other structured personality inventories, measures of scalability are likely to be related to each other and to moderate predictability for traits in the domain of conscientiousness. The beneficial effects of the moderator are likely to be greatest for low scalability individuals initially in the "off-quadrants," or for whom predictor and target scores are dissimilar.

8

Scalability Re-examined

This book began with a restatement of the obvious: Trait words, used properly, can map on to personality structures, and so can explain behavior. In this chapter, I will review the empirical studies of Chapters 4 - 7 and re-examine my theoretical position in light of these findings. This leads to the description of an additional empirical study, in which I investigate the utility of measuring scalability in the domain of *authoritarianism*. I conclude by briefly considering the context of scalability in the discipline of personality psychology, and, moreover, by evaluating the tension between quantitative and idiographic approaches to the psychology of personality.

8.1 Review of findings

In the empirical studies of chapters 4, 6, and 7, measures of scalability have been evaluated on samples totalling 680 subjects. (An additional 254 subjects participated in pretesting). What are the lessons of these investigations?

8.1.1 Moderator effects

The focus of my empirical studies, like those that preceded this work, has been on the role of scalability as a moderator in prediction. Examined globally, the results do not appear encouraging: Most of the increments in R^2 attributable to moderator effects are in the range of .01 - .03. From a practical standpoint, measures of scalability are unlikely to substantially increase sample-wide predictability for most traits.

A casual examination of the moderator effects shown in Tables 6.8 and 7.4 reveals that these are statistically significant in only a handful of cases. But significance tests of moderator effects may be inappropriate (Tisak, 1988). Moreover, there is a definite patterning in the results, one that is supported also by investigations of other approaches to measuring consistency. Other studies have typically reported a modest effect of consistency in the domain of conscientiousness (e.g., Bem & Allen, 1974; Chaplin & Goldberg, 1984; Lanning, 1988; Mischel & Peake, 1982). For other traits, null results have generally been found, except where very large samples have been employed (e.g., Zuckerman et al., 1988).

For the trait of achievement in the SBI study, five of the six tests of moderator effects showed substantial effects in the predicted direction; the sixth result was essentially null (Table 6.8). In the study of scalability on personality inventories, additional support was found for the hypothesized moderator effect in the area of school achievement. Because achievement is in the same broad domain as conscientiousness, (Digman, 1990), these results support the hypothesis that consistency will moderate prediction in the domain of conscientiousness. This convergence occurred despite the differences between the scalability approach and other approaches used to measure consistency.

Outside of the domain of conscientiousness, the moderator effects found in the SBI study are unstable over the various target measures, and so appear attributable to chance. The picture is similar for the study of scalability on personality inventories: For the measure of school achievement, the effect size for the scalability moderator term was .14, but for the remaining traits, effect sizes ranged from -.06 to +.07.

In short, differences in scale content appear largely sufficient to account for the pattern of moderator findings. Nonetheless, several conjectures can be made about relations between formal aspects of measures and moderator effects. The first is that stronger results will be obtained for instruments with situation-behavior formats such as the SBI than when more traditional instruments are used. The second is that on standard personality inventories, results will be stronger where scales are *not* highly homogeneous, such as on the CPI, than where scales are highly internally consistent, as on the MPQ.

Is sample-wide predictability the only criterion? It can be argued that the search for moderator effects is unlikely to reap substantial rewards. Because simple linear effects are both powerful and robust, moderator effects are unlikely to contribute importantly to sample-wide prediction.

However, two reasons may be cited why this does *not* imply that investigations of consistency as a moderator are misguided. The first is empirical. As seen in Chapter 7, moderator effects will differ from person to person in a sample. Consequently, a small sample-wide effect may mask important results at the level of the individual. Levine and his colleagues argue that these individual differences, coupled with the insensitivity of correlations to non-linear effects, renders the multiple regression approach inappropriate as a test of individual differences in test consistency (Hulin, Drasgow, & Parsons, 1983).

The second reason is more conceptual. Increasing sample-wide predictability is an important goal in the field, but it is not the only goal. R^2 increments are not the *sine qua non* of basic research: Investigations which seek to further understanding through the refinement of theory and the opening of new topics cannot be evaluated on the basis of a single applied criterion.

For these reasons, it would be premature to abandon the investigation of theory-sanctioned moderators of prediction, including scalability as well as other ostensive measures of consistency.

8.1.2 Other results

Although most of my discussion has been focussed on the presence or absence of moderator effects, a number of additional findings have been reported. These are sampled below:

First, many measures of scalability and elevation on situation-behavior inventories are sufficiently independent so that both approaches can in principle be useful (Chapters 4 and 6). Further, measures of scalability can be reliable (Chapters 4, 6, and 7). However, it remains unclear whether the reliable variance in measures of scalability is unique, that is, independent of elevation.

Second, measures of scalability may contribute in two ways to the prediction of target variables. The moderator, or indirect role has been considered at length. Direct relations between scalability and target measures may also be informative. For example, among women in the SBI study, scalability for the trait of conscientiousness was directly associated with higher scores on all three target variables, and two of these relations were statistically significant (Table 6.8).

Third, on personality inventories, measures of scalability on different traits appear to be highly related, and to tap a theme of generalized norm-sensitivity (Chapter 7).

Fourth, the difficulties involved in constructing an ecologically valid situation-behavior inventory are, I think, instructive. If naturalistic data are to be used as the raw material upon which an inventory is built, then the paper-and-pencil descriptions of most situations will require the addition of a note of conflict if these items are to be informative about individual differences in personality. A stickier problem is that the formalism of this approach is limiting in several respects: If a multi-trait situation-behavior inventory is to be both realistic and useful, different response options should probably be provided for each item. Unfortunately, as the scale values for the behaviors are context-dependent, the scoring of such an instrument becomes highly problematic.

Fifth, in spite of the limitations of the SBI, some of the descriptive statistics for this measure are worth noting. For example, over a set of items designed to be representative of undergraduate life, the most popular response option *(Help or cooperate with them)* described cooperative, group-centered behavior (Figure 6.1). Despite the cultural narcissism of the times, subjects were far less likely to choose socially desirable items with a more agentic tone such as *Take the initiative yourself* or *Act responsibly*. It is possible that this apparent aspiration towards cooperation is partially attributable to the unusual good-naturedness of the small pretest sample which generated the original SBI item pool (Chapter 5). It remains, however, that the relative frequencies of the items counter-indicates *self-centered* as a normative descriptor of the Berkeley undergraduate in the mid 1980s.

8.2 Traits reconsidered

It is appropriate to re-examine the conceptual roots of the scalability approach presented in the first few chapters in light of the subsequent empirical findings.

If one is concerned with measurement, two questions about personality traits stand out as particularly worthy of investigation. The first of these addresses the meaning of trait words, the second is concerned with which trait words are particularly worthy of study.

8.2.1 What do trait words mean?

In completely general terms, a trait word can only refer to a pattern of behavior in situation. Evidently, a "pattern" might consist of a single event - as, for example, murder renders one *homicidal*. Or, a pattern might consist of a frequent pattern of behavior, manifested without regard to the situation. As a pervasive tendency to fall asleep might characterize the *narcoleptic*, so a similar tendency towards anxiety describes the *neurotic*.

This simple frequency approach is powerful and attractive. But many of the more interesting and informative traits of personality seem to describe situation-contingent behavior. When we are told, for example, that Eddie, age 10, is a terror, and picks fights with the other children, we do know that Eddie is manifestly aggressive. But we don't know if this is caused by boredom, family environment, a family trauma such as a divorce, or even too much sugar in his diet. When we are told that Willie, also 10, is a terror at school, but an "angel" at home, I would argue that we know something far more important about Willie, his family life, and the man that he will eventually become (Allport, 1961; Block, 1968). Even broadband traits such as neuroticism are best understood when one goes beyond simple counts and seeks a deeper level than is afforded by the summary view (e.g., Shapiro, 1965, 1981).

The patterning of behavior is only "inconsistent" when viewed at a level of trivializing superficiality. The situation-contingent patterning of behavior points towards, and not away from, enduring and potentially explanatory personality structures. Our attention should not be focussed on whether "consistency" exists, but on what patterns to look for, or what traits to study.

8.2.2 What trait words should be studied?

There has been no issue in the field in recent years which has attracted as much attention as the question of which trait words to study. I find this somewhat ironic, for in reviewing my empirical work, my sense is that I have paid too much attention to formal and epistemological questions, and insufficient attention to this question of substance.

In the contemporary literature, the modal solution to the question of "what to measure" is the five-factor model of Tupes and Christal (1961) and many others. Digman (1990) has recently described these factors as Extraversion/introversion (or Surgency), Friendliness/hostility (or Agreeableness), Conscientiousness (or Will to Achieve), Neuroticism/emotional stability, and Intellect (or Openness). The factors are of undeniable importance: When a large sample of individuals is rated using a set of trait terms sampled representatively from the lexicon, this five dimensional model appears adequate for describing relations among these terms (see John, Angleitner, & Ostendorf, 1988, for a recent review).

In spite of the appeal and elegance of the five-factor model, several limitations should be noted. First, the model is inherently descriptive, concerned more with the psychology of lay attribution than with finding an approach for the optimal characterization of personality. Second, there is no logical link between the eigenstructure of a normative correlation matrix and the psychological "structures" that, I would argue, we are ultimately concerned with (Guilford, 1975; Lanning & Gough, 1990). Third, because the model is nomothetic, it is compromised by the possibility that the trait words that are useful for describing everyone will not optimally characterize any particular individuals. Fourth, there are other approaches to the question of which trait words to study - such as Gough's folk concept approach (Gough, 1987), the expert judge approach used by Block in constructing the California Q-set (Block, 1961/1978), and evolutionary approaches (Buss, 1988) - and the commensurateness of these various solutions is by no means absolute (Lanning & Gough, 1990).

8.3 Scalability and authoritarianism: Rationale

Where is scalability likely to contribute to the measurement of personality dispositions? Tellegen (1988) has recently argued that measures of individual differences in consistency are most likely to be useful in measuring higher-order traits or structures. Tellegen described these as *master schemata*, and used Loevinger's concept of ego development as a case in point. Tellegen cites the study of Haan, Stroud and Holstein (1973), which found that the responses of a sample of "hippies" could be best described in Loevinger's system, as conformist. This result appears paradoxical when viewed superficially, but the "paradox" is resolved by distinguishing between manifest behavior and the underlying schema or construct. That is, although the sample of hippies appeared manifestly and avowedly non-conformist, the issue of conformity *versus* non-conformity remained focal in their experience. Tellegen described the manifest conformity as "B-conformity" (for behavioral conformity), as opposed to the S-conformity (for schema-conformity). In the present language, I would suggest that the hippies were highly scalable for the dimension of conformity, but low on elevation for this dimension.

Loevinger's concept of ego development grew out of her earlier work on authoritarian family ideology (Ernhart & Loevinger, 1969; see Loevinger, 1987, chapter 6). In the following section, I articulate several reasons why authoritarianism appears to be an appropriate domain for assessing scalability.

8.3.1 Authoritarianism as a schema

It is self-evident that authoritarianism is important in human behavior. From a political and sociological standpoint, writers have long been drawn to the question of how totalitarian regimes can come into being (e.g., Fromm, 1932; cited in Samelson, 1986). From a psychological standpoint, we are drawn to the question of how the initially powerless child grows to understand and internalize the ubiquitous presence of authority in her or his life (e.g., Adorno et al., 1950).

Today, authoritarianism remains an important area of investigation among sociologists, political scientists and political psychologists, but it is little studied among personality and social psychologists. The topic is neglected in spite of its continued importance, an importance which is testified to by increasing response rates for most statements characteristic of authoritarian attitudes in recent years (Altemeyer, 1988).

Most conceptions of authoritarianism are multi-faceted, seeing authoritarianism as not one trait, but several. In *The Authoritarian Personality*, Sanford described authoritarianism as consisting of nine components, including conventionalism, authoritarian submission, authoritarian aggression, anti-intraception (an unwillingness to introspect or to consider motives), superstition/stereotypy, power/toughness, destructiveness/cynicism, projectivity, and preoccupation with sex. Following a series of careful analyses, Altemeyer (1988) has argued that only the first three of these traits - conventionalism, authoritarian submission, and authoritarian aggression - show substantial covariation.

In spite of the relative parsimony and greater psychometric sophistication of recent approaches, these remain limited in that authoritarianism is still seen as a cluster of social attitudes which lie "on the surface," (Adorno et al, p. 3), rather than as a single schema or structure which "lies behind behavior and within the individual" (Adorno et al., p. 5). Ideally, a single, fundamental principle could be identified which lies at the core of authoritarianism.

One possibility is straightforward: The authoritarian perceives and responds to the world in terms of status and authority. More explicitly, we expect the authoritarian to be deferential to persons perceived to be of high status and aggressive to persons perceived to be of low status. The non-authoritarian, by way of contrast, sees the world in terms of other dimensions.

8.3.2 Authoritarianism and the interpersonal circumplex

If the authoritarian sees the world in terms of status, what dimension is he or she neglecting? Alternatively, if status is the orienting concept of social interaction for the authoritarian, then what concepts might govern the interpersonal world of the non-authoritarian?

A large body of theory and research testifies to the utility of a two dimensional interpretation of interpersonal behavior, with the two axes defined by the exchange of status/control and love/affiliation (e.g., Carson, 1969; Kiesler, 1983; Leary, 1957; Wiggins, 1982). This two dimensional model is known as the interpersonal circumplex; it is based on the hypothesis that love and status are the basic commodities of social exchange (e.g., Foa, 1966).

Linking the research on the interpersonal circumplex to the study of authoritarianism, we expect that the commodity of status will be salient to the authoritarian, and that he or she will be disproportionately sensitive to status in interpersonal interactions. The non-authoritarian, by contrast, will be relatively neglectful of and insensitive to status. The interpersonal behavior of such persons will appear to be governed by love rather than status, by affective, rather than pragmatic, concerns.

8.4 Scalability and authoritarianism: Reanalysis of the SBI data

In this section, I describe a pilot study in which the Berkeley SBI data are reanalyzed for the trait of authoritarian deference. More specifically, these data are scored for the extent to which deferential responding was selectively associated with items in which antagonists were adults rather than peers. This "selective deference" index is then related to self and peer ratings of authoritarianism on the Adjective Check List (ACL; Gough & Heilbrun, 1983). Following description of this and additional, exploratory analyses, I consider the utility of this conception of authoritarianism.

8.4.1 The Berkeley SBI study

The Situation-Behavior Inventory (SBI) is a research instrument used to assess individual differences in scalability on a variety of traits in samples of college students; the measure is included in Appendix 1, and its development is described at length in Chapter 5. In Chapter 6, I described the administration of the SBI to a sample of 115 male and 89 female University of California undergraduates. These subjects also completed the Adjective Check List (ACL). For most subjects (N = 132, 65% of sample), a peer also rated the subject using the ACL.

8.4.2 Scaling of behaviors

For the reanalysis of the SBI data, a new set of scale values for the response options was required. Accordingly, a sample of 71 Oregon State University undergraduates rated the 18 SBI response options for the trait of deference. Deference was defined in the course of the following instructions:

> When two people have conflicting goals, and one person allows the other to take control of the situation, we say that the first person has *acted deferentially* and *respectfully*. When people yield to others, and let others make decisions, we say that these people have deferred. When they grant power and status to others, we say that they have acted respectfully.
>
> The opposite of deference and respect is *resistance* and *disrespect*. When people do not yield, and insist on making their own decisions, we say that these people have *resisted*; when they withhold power and status from others, we say that they have acted disrespectfully.
>
> As you can imagine, deference and respect are very important parts of social interaction. In this study, we are trying to understand more about deference and respect.

Subjects rated the SBI using a 1 (*This type of behavior is very strongly resistant/disrespectful*) to 7 (*This type of behavior is very strongly deferential/respectful*) scale. Results are described in Table 8.1.

TABLE 8.1 - MEAN RATINGS OF 18 BEHAVIORS FOR AUTHORITARIAN DEFERENCE

Mean	S.D.	Behavior
5.69	1.00	Help or cooperate with them.
5.42	1.50	Act responsibly; do the right thing.
5.26	0.97	Ask (someone) for help.
4.94	1.16	Get together with friends.
4.68	1.13	Ask why; get more information.
4.61	1.86	Persist, work until it is done or correct.
4.49	1.30	Not take it personally; forget it.
4.44	1.13	Relax, rest, or take a break.
4.38	1.14	Do something flirtatious, romantic, or erotic.
4.25	1.02	Feel embarrassed, blush, or be tongue-tied.
4.03	1.89	Take the initiative yourself.
4.01	1.40	Work or study (alone).
3.72	1.40	Cry; express distress.
3.66	1.31	Remind them about what they should do.
3.63	1.39	Take it personally; feel hurt.
3.42	1.46	Be frank and say you can't help them.
3.25	1.75	Give up, do something else.
3.20	1.21	Get upset; express frustration.

Note: N = 70 - 71 undergraduates.

8.4.3 Scoring

Self and peer ACLs were scored for a balanced-key 24 item scale designed to measure authoritarianism. Positive items on this scale were *aggressive*, *arrogant*, *cold*, *cynical*, *distrustful*, *dominant*, *fearful*, *hostile*, *intolerant*, *prejudiced*, *rigid*, and *submissive*. Negative items included *affectionate*, *courageous*, *emotional*, *gentle*, *individualistic*, *informal*, *rebellious*, *sensitive*, *sympathetic*, *tolerant*, *trusting*, and *warm*.

Rather than rely on the sample data for estimates of item evocativeness, the 102 items of the SBI were instead coded rationally into one of three categories, based on the apparent status level of the antagonist in the interaction. The first category included interactions with adults, such as professors, parents, and landlords; 25 items were assigned into this category. The second category included the 14 items which describe interactions with peers other than close friends (e.g. roommates, acquaintances, strangers). The remaining 65 items included descriptions of situations which were not interpersonal as well as seemingly egalitarian interactions between close friends; these were not scored in this analysis.

After the adult and peer items were coded using the ratings shown in Table 8.1, an index of "selective deference" was computed by simply subtracting the average level of deference in responses to the peer items from the average level of deference in response to the adult items.

8.4.4 Results

In the combined sample, correlations between the selective deference index and the target measure of ACL authoritarianism were statistically significant for both the peer ACL ($r = .24, p < .05$) and the self-report ACL ($r = .15, p < .05$). Within-sex results were quite similar, with self and peer correlations of .20 and .19 for the male sample and .14 and .33 for the female sample.

Though these correlations are modest in size, additional results support the discriminant validity of the selective deference index and its interpretation as a measure of authoritarianism: In the peer data, the selective deference index was more strongly related to ACL authoritarianism than to any of the 37 standard ACL scales; in the self-report data, only the *Need for Nurturance* and *Need for Affiliation* scales exceeded the correlation obtained by the selective deference index (the value of both of these correlations was -.16).

To further understand the selective deference index, I also assessed relations between it and the individual items of the ACL. Given the inherent limitations of single items, and the relatively small number of cases for the peer data, it is evident that these should be interpreted with caution.

In the peer ACL data, the strongest correlates were as follows (all $p < .05$).

Positive:

Hurried, Prejudiced, Distrustful, Affected, Coarse, Loud, Arrogant

Negative:

Trusting, Friendly, Stingy, Poised, Complicated, Forgiving, Independent, Pleasant, Undependable

The adjectives give additional support to the hypothesis that selective deference on the SBI is associated with the pattern of skepticism and social coldness traditionally considered to be part of the authoritarian syndrome.

The self-report correlates are listed below (again, all $p < .05$):

Positive

Unassuming, Pessimistic, Talkative, Stubborn, Outspoken, Fault-finding, Frivolous, Flirtatious, Dissatisfied, Hard-headed, Fickle, Nagging, Impatient, Smug

Negative

Active, Patient, Affectionate, Modest, Praising, Rude

Although these are clearly not as coherent as the peer data, the overall pattern does not counter-indicate the validity of the SBI measure of selective deference.

Finally, to assess the utility of the conception of authoritarianism as a situation (or item) contingent pattern of responding, I also computed an index of overall deference, by summing the average deference exhibited in the adult and peer items. This was unrelated to the target measure of authoritarianism in both the self report ACL data (r = .05) and peer data (r = -.08). In the self report data, the highest correlation between the ACL scales and this summary index of deference was -.12 for the ACL femininity scale; in the peer data, the highest correlation was .22 with the A-4 scale, which describes low origence/high intellectence (Gough & Heilbrun, 1983).

8.4.5 Implications

The SBI authoritarianism index is technically not a measure of scalability, but it is similar, differing essentially in that the evocativeness values for the situations are assigned rationally (e.g., 1 for adult, 0 for peer) rather than empirically. The correlates of this measure support the hypothesis that authoritarianism refers to a pattern of behavior, or an interaction between a variable describing situations (specifically, the status of other interactants) and a variable describing behavior (scale values for deference).

The present interpretation of authoritarianism may have implications for the recent controversy in the literature concerning complementarity in interpersonal behavior. Both Carson and Kiesler have asserted that interpersonal behavior is complementary, that is, that exchanges of love are correspondent (love evokes love, and hate evokes hate) and that exchanges of status are reciprocal (dominance evokes submission and submission evokes dominance). But the empirical support for this last proposition has been inconsistent, and so Orford (1986) has argued that dominance evokes submission only under certain conditions. The present model predicts that dominance will evoke submission only for some persons, namely, authoritarians. Consequently, the validity of the interpersonal complementarity hypothesis will depend upon the sample studied.

Additional investigations of this conception of authoritarianism are presently under way (Lanning, 1990).

8.5 Towards reconciliation of psychometric and idiographic approaches to personality

Over the years, investigators have repeatedly drawn a distinction between two approaches to psychology. Murray (Murray et al., 1938) distinguished between the centralist and peripheralist camps. Allport (1955) contrasted Leibnizian and Lockean approaches. Thorndike (1954) found a psychometric *versus* verbal factor, Ansbacher (1961) described the holistic and the elementary views, and Coan's (1968) scaling of psychological theories led to the two categories of *fluid* (synthetic) *versus restrictive* (analytic).[1] William James (1890) was one of the few to recognize the virtues of both positions, which he later characterized as tough-minded and tender-minded (James, 1907). It would be inaccurate to say that James truly transcended this dichotomy; rather, here as elsewhere, he sequentially embraced both positions (Allport, 1943).

It is instructive to place these two approaches on a single continuum, and then to use this dimension to characterize theorists rather than theories. When one does this, the pathologies that characterize both endpoints appear familiar. The fluid thinker maintains a diffuse, global and impressionistic appreciation of the big picture; but this may ultimately preclude factual knowledge as the inspiring visionary drifts towards the complete incoherence of the *hysteric*. Similarly, the analytically-inclined maintain the risk of methodological dogmatism, rigidity, and the utter loss of perspective that is the hallmark of the *obsessive-compulsive* (Shapiro, 1965).

In the psychology of personality, the synthetic position may be fairly characterized as *idiographic* - the emoting, striving person is *the* big picture. It would seem to follow that the analytic position could be described as nomothetic, however, many who embrace the nomothetic approach are better characterized as pragmatic rather than analytic (see Chapter 1). Instead, *psychometric* is an accurate description of the analytic orientation in personality psychology.

The virtues of the idiographic and psychometric positions frequently appear to be lost on those who embrace the opposing viewpoint (Cronbach, 1954). This is unfortunate, for the idiographic position would benefit from the rigor of psychometrics, and the psychometric approach would similarly benefit from the perspective of the idiographer. For this reason, it is worthwhile to seek to combine the strengths of the two views (Simonton, 1989).

8.5.1 To what extent is scalability an idiographic approach?

There is a tremendous gap between, on the one hand, an array of trait words and associated scalability scores and, on the other, a stirring biography or case study. For this reason, several investigators have argued that the use of consistency as a moderator variable is not an idiographic method (e.g., Mischel & Peake, 1982; Paunonen & Jackson, 1985). But in focussing on the

---

[1] For readers who are unclear about their own approach, I would suggest that those who resist the equating of the various dichotomies fall into the second camp, and that those who do not fall in to the first.

difference between case studies and statistical methods, these investigators have failed to recognize that there is an important distinction between consistency measurement and traditional approaches, in that only the former seeks to understand trait relevance.

The relevance of trait relevance. Consider the freshman student who appears equally extraverted and conscientious. When confronted with a situation such as "a party during finals week," the student appears pulled towards two incompatible behaviors. The behavior he or she chooses in this situation is not predictable from traditional scores on the two traits, but it is also not random. If we wished to predict behavior in this situation, we would want to know whether the observed extraversion reflected a profound need for companionship, or if it was instead essentially in the service of other needs. We would ask similar questions about the manifest conscientiousness: Is this internalized and subjectively important, or simply a cluster of superficial habits carried over from life in the parental home? We would ask these questions because they provide an index of the subjective relevance of the two trait words for the individual.

The concept of trait relevance will appear foreign to those who embrace the biosocial or constructive viewpoint: If traits are merely normative dimensions upon which persons can be compared, then persons cannot differ in trait relevance. But, as we have seen, the biosocial perspective is incomplete (Chapter 1). Personality assessment can be profitably understood as a mapping process which links the two domains of language and psyche. On this perspective, trait relevance provides a measure of the correspondence between the intrinsically normative trait word and the intrapsychic dispositions of the actor.

Trait relevance is not assessed by the summary approach to measurement. A normative, summary score on a trait does not provide an index of the relevance of the trait for the individual; as Lamiell (1982) has argued, the notion that our behavior is determined by our normative standing on a trait is logically incoherent.

The scalability method is a simple and conceptually attractive approach to assessing individual differences in trait relevance. For a few trait words, such as *authoritarian* and *achieving*, measures of trait relevance appear empirically as well as conceptually promising, and assessing scalability may lead to improvements in both prediction and understanding. For most trait words, scalability will not moderate sample-wide predictability, but still may provide insights into some of the persons we measure.

References

Adorno, T. W., Frenkel-Brunswik, E., Levinson, D.J., & Sanford, R.N. (1950). *The Authoritarian Personality*. New York: Harper.

Alker, H. A. (1972). Is personality situationally specific or intrapsychically consistent? *Journal of Personality, 40*, 1-16.

Allport, G. W. (1937). *Personality: A psychological interpretation.* New York: Holt.

Allport, G. W. (1943). The productive paradoxes of William James. *Psychological Review, 50*, 451-478.

Allport, G. W. (1955). *Becoming: Basic considerations for a psychology of personality.* New Haven: Yale University Press.

Allport, G. W. (1961). *Pattern and Growth in Personality*. New York: Holt.

Allport, G. W. (Ed). (1965). *Letters from Jenny*. NY: Harcourt Brace

Allport, G. W. (1966). Traits revisited. *American Psychologist, 21*, 1-10.

Allport, G. W., & Vernon, P. (1933). *Studies in expressive movement*. N.Y.: MacMillan.

Altemeyer, B. (1988). *Enemies of Freedom: Understanding Right-Wing Authoritarianism.* San Francisco: Jossey-Bass.

Althauser, R. P. (1971). Multicollinearity and non-additive regression rules. In H. Blalock (Ed.), *Causal models in the social sciences* (p. 453-472). . Chicago: Aldine-Atherton.

American Psychiatric Association (1980). *Diagnostic and Statistical Manual of Mental Disorders (3rd Ed.)* Washington, D.C.: Author

Ansbacher, H. L. (1961). On the origin of holism. *Journal of Individual Psychology, 17*, 142-148.

Argyle, M., Furnham, A., & Graham, J. A. (1981). *Social Situations*. Cambridge: Cambridge University Press.

Argyle, M., & Little, B. R. (1972). Do personality traits apply to social behavior? *Journal for the Theory of Social Behavior, 2*, 1-35.

Averill, J. R. (1973). The dis-position of psychological dispositions. *Journal of Experimental Research in Personality*, 6, 275-282.

Baumeister, R. F., & Tice, D. M. (1988). Metatraits. *Journal of Personality, 56*, 1-40.

Bem, D. J. (1983). Further deja vu in the search for cross-situational consistency: A response to Mischel and Peake. *Psychological Review, 90*, 390-393.

Bem, D. J., & Allen, A. (1974). On predicting some of the people some of the time: The search for cross-situational consistencies in behavior. *Psychological Review, 81*, 506-520.

Bem, S. L. (1981). Gender schema theory: A cognitive account of sex-typing. *Psychological Review, 88*, 354-364.

Berdie, R. F. (1961). Intra-individual variability and predictability. *Educational and Psychological Measurement, 21*, 663-676.

Berdie, R. F. (1969). Consistency and generalizability of intraindividual variability. *Journal of Applied Psychology, 53,* 35-41. [a]

Berdie, R. F. (1969). Intra-individual temporal variability and predictability. *Educational and Psychological Measurement, 29,* 235-257. [b]

Bishop, D. W., & Witt, P. A. (1970). Sources of behavioral variance during leisure time. *Journal of Personality and Social Psychology, 16*, 352-360

Block, J. (1961). Ego identity, role variability, and adjustment. *Journal of Consulting Psychology*, *25*, 392-397.

Block, J. (1962). *The California Q-set*. Palo Alto, CA: Consulting Psychologists Press.

Block, J. (1968). Some reasons for the apparent inconsistency of personality. *Psychological Bulletin*, *70*, 210-212.

Block, J. (1989). A critique of the act frequency approach to personality. *Journal of Personality and Social Psychology*, *56*, 234-245.

Block, J. H., & Block, J. (1980). The role of ego-control and ego-resiliency in the organization of behavior. In Collins, (Ed.). *Development of cognition, affect, and social relations: The Minnesota symposia on child psychology, vol. 13.* Hillsdale, NJ: Erlbaum.

Block, J., Weiss, D. W., & Thorne, A. (1979). How relevant is a semantic similarity interpretation of personality ratings? *Journal of Personality and Social Psychology*, *37*, 1055-1074.

Bruner, J. S., Goodnow, J. J., & Austin, G. A. (1956). *A study of thinking*. N.Y.: Wiley

Burke, P. A., Kraut, R. E., & Dworkin, R. H. (1984). Traits, consistency, and self-schemata: What do our methods measure? *Journal of Personality and Social Psychology*, *47*, 568-579.

Buss, A. H. (1988). *Personality: Evolutionary heritage and human distinctiveness.* Hillsdale, NJ: Erlbaum.

Buss, A. H., & Durkee, A. (1957). An inventory for assessing different kinds of hostility. *Journal of Consulting and Clinical Psychology* , *21*, 343-349.

Buss, A. H., & Plomin, R. (1975). *A temperament theory of personality development.* NY: Wiley.

Buss, D. M. & Craik, K. H. (1980). The frequency concept of disposition: Dominance and prototypically dominant acts. *Journal of Personality*, *51*, 401-408.

Buss, D. M., & Craik, K. H. (1983). The act frequency approach to personality. *Psychological Review*, *90*, 105-126.

Buss, D. M., & Craik, K. H. (1984). *The act frequency approach and the construction of personality*. Paper presented at the Second European Conference on Personality Psychology, Bielefeld, Germany, May 16-19, 1984.

Buss, D. M., & Craik, K. H. (1985). Why not measure that trait? Alternative criteria for identifying important dispositions. *Journal of Personality and Social Psychology*, *48*, 934-946.

Campus, N. (1974). Transsituational consistency as a dimension of personality. *Journal of Personality and Social Psychology*, *29*, 593-600.

Carlson, R. (1984). What's social about social psychology? Where's the person in personality research? *Journal of Personality and Social Psychology* , *47*, 1304-1309.

Carson, R. C. (1969). *Interaction concepts of personality*. Chicago: Aldine.

Cattell, R. B. (1943). Fluctuation of sentiments and attitudes as a measure of character integration and of temperament. *American Journal of Psychology*, *56*, 195-216.

Cattell, R. B. (1946). *The description and measurement of personality* NY: World Book.

Cattell, R. B. (1983). *Structured personality-learning theory: A wholistic multivariate approach*. N. Y.: Praeger

Chaplin, W. F., & Goldberg, L. R. (1984). A failure to replicate the Bem and Allen study of individual differences in cross-situational consistency. *Journal of Personality and Social Psychology*, *47*, 1074-1090.

Chaplin, W. F., & Locklear, T. S. (1988). *The convergence between self and other personality ratings: Construct similarity as a moderator variable.* Paper presented at the 96th Annual Convention of the American Psychological Association, Atlanta, August 12, 1988.

Cheek, J. M. (1982). Aggregation, moderator variables, and the validity of personality tests: A peer-rating study. *Journal of Personality and Social Psychology, 43*, 1254-1269.

Coan, R. W. (1968). Dimensions of psychological theory. *American Psychologist, 23*, 715-722.

Cohen, L. J. (1977). *The probable and the provable*. Oxford: Clarendon.

Cohen, J. (1978). Partialed products *are* interactions; Partialed powers *are* curve components. *Psychological Bulletin, 85*, 858-866.

Cohen, J. & Cohen, P. (1975). *Applied multiple regression/correlation analysis for the behavioral sciences*. Hillsdale, NJ: Erlbaum.

Conley, J. J. (1985). A personality theory of adulthood and aging. In R. Hogan & W. H. Jones (Eds.), *Perspectives in Personality, Volume 1*. Greenwich, CT: JAI.

Cronbach, L. J. (1954). Report on a psychometric mission to clinicia. *Psychometrika, 19*, 263-270.

Cronbach, L. J. (1987). Statistical tests for moderator variables: Flaws in analyses recently proposed. *Psychological Bulletin, 102*, 414-417.

Cronbach, L. J., Gleser, G. C., Nanda, H., & Rajaratnam, N. (1972). *The dependability of behavioral measurements*. N. Y.: Wiley.

Cronbach, L. J., & Meehl, P.E. (1955). Construct validity in psychological tests. *Psychological Bulletin*, 1955, *52*, 281-302.

Digman, J. M. (1990). Personality structure: Emergence of the five-factor model. *Annual Review of Psychology, 41*, 417-440.

Digman, J. M., & Inouye, J. (1986). Further specification of the five robust factors of personality. *Journal of Personality and Social Psychology, 50*, 116-123.

Donlon, T. F., & Fischer, F. E. (1968). An index of an individual's agreement with group determined item difficulties. *Educational and Psychological Measurement, 28*, 105-113.

Drasgow, F., Levine, M. V. & Williams, E. A. (1985). Appropriateness measurement with polychotomous item response models and standardized indices. *British Journal of Mathematical and Statistical Psychology, 38*, 67-86.

Dworkin, R. H., & Kihlstrom, J. F. (1977). An S-R inventory of dominance for research on the nature of person-situation interactions. *Journal of Personality, 45*, 43-55.

Edwards, A. L. (1957). *Manual for the Edwards Personal Preference Schedule*. New York: Psychological Corporation.

Endler, N. S. & Hunt, J. McV. (1966). Sources of behavioral variance as measured by the S-R inventory of anxiousness. *Psychological Bulletin, 65*, 336-346.

Endler, N. S., & Hunt, J. McV. (1969). S-R Inventories of Hostility and comparisons of the proportions of variance from persons, responses, and situations for Hostility and Anxiousness. *Journal of Personality and Social Psychology , 37*, 1-24.

Endler, N. S., Hunt, J. McV., & Rosenstein, S. (1962). An S-R inventory of Anxiousness. *Psychological Monographs, 76*, 1-33. (Whole No. 536).

Endler, N. S. & Magnusson, D. (1976). Personality and person by situation interactions. In N. S. Endler & D. Magnusson (Eds.), *Interactional psychology and personality*. Washington: Hemisphere. [a]

Endler, N. S., & Magnusson, D. (1976). *Interactional psychology and personality.* Washington, D. C.: Hemisphere. [b]

Epstein, S. (1979). The stability of behavior: I. On predicting most of the people much of the time. *Journal of Personality and Social Psychology, 37,* 1097-1126.

Erdelyi, M. H. (1974). A new look at the New Look: Perceptual defense and vigilance. *Psychological Review, 81,* 1-25.

Erikson, E. H. (1950). *Childhood and Society.* New York: Norton.

Ernhart, C. B., & Loevinger, J. (1969) Authoritarian family ideology: A measure, its correlates, and its robustness. *Multivariate Behavioral Research Monographs.* (Whole No. 69-1),

Eysenck, H. J. (1969). *Personality structure and measurement.* San Diego: Knapp.

Eysenck, H. J. (1970). Explanation and the concept of personality. In R. Borger & F. Cioffi (Eds.), *Explanation in the Behavioural Sciences* (pp. 387-410). Cambridge: Cambridge University Press.

Fenigstein, A., Scheier, M. F., & Buss, A. H. (1975). Public and private self-consciousness: Assessment and theory. *Journal of Consulting and Clinical Psychology, 43,* 522-527.

Feshbach, S. & Weiner, B. (1986). *Personality (2nd Ed.).* Lexington, MA: D.C. Heath.

Fiske, D. W. (1957). The constraints on intra-individual variability in test responses. *Educational and Psychological Measurement, 17,* 317-337.

Fiske, D. W. (1963). Homogeneity and variation in measuring personality. *American Psychologist, 18,* 643-652.

Fiske, D. W. (1974). The limits for the conventional science of personality. *Journal of Personality, 47,* 136-161.

Fiske, D. W. and Rice, L. (1955). Intra-individual response variability. *Psychological Bulletin,* 52, 217-250.

Foa, U. G. (1966). Perception of behavior in reciprocal roles: The ringex model. *Psychological Monographs: General and Applied, 80* (Whole No. 623).

Fromm, E. (1932). Die psychoanalytische Charakterologie und ihre Bedeutung fuer die Sozial psychologie. *Zeitschrift fuer Sozialforschung, 1,* 253-277.

Funder, D. C., & Ozer, D. J. (1983). Behavior as a function of the situation. *Journal of Personality and Social Psychology, 44,* 107-112.

Funder, D. C. (1983). Three issues in predicting more of the people: A reply to Mischel and Peake. *Psychological Review, 90,* 283-289.

Ghiselli, E. E. (1960). The prediction of predictability. *Educational and Psychological Measurement, 20,* 3-8.

Ghiselli, E. E. (1963). Moderating effects and differential reliability and validity. *Journal of Applied Psychology , 47,* 81-86.

Glaser, R. (1952). The reliability of inconsistency. *Educational and Psychological Measurement, 12,* 60-64.

Goldberg, L. R. (1978). The reliability of reliability: The generality and correlates of intra-individual consistency in responses to structured personality inventories. *Applied Psychological Measurement, 2,* 269-291.

Goldberg, L. R. (1982). From Ace to Zombie: Some explorations in the language of personality, In C. D. Spielberger & J. N. Butcher, (Eds.), *Advances in Personality Assessment* (Volume 1, p. 203-234). Hillsdale, NJ: Erlbaum.

Golding, S. L. (1975). Flies in the ointment: Methodological problems in the analysis of the percentage of variance due to persons and situations. *Psychological Bulletin, 82,* 272-288.

Golding, S. L. (1978). Toward a more adequate theory of personality: Psychological organizing principles. In H. London (Ed.), *Personality: A new look at metatheories.* New York: Wiley.

Gough, H. G. (1960). The theory and measurement of socialization. *Journal of Consulting Psychology, 24*, 23-30.

Gough, H. G. (1965). Conceptual analysis of psychological test scores and other diagnostic variables. *Journal of Abnormal Psychology, 70*, 294-302.

Gough, H. G. (1971). Some reflections on the meaning of psychodiagnosis. *American Psychologist, 26*, 160-167.

Gough, H. G. (1975). *Manual for the California Psychological Inventory. (Rev. Ed.)*. Palo Alto, CA: Consulting Psychologists press.

Gough, H. G. (1987). *California Psychological Inventory Administrator's Guide*. Palo Alto, CA: Consulting Psychologists Press.

Gough, H. G., & Heilbrun, A. B. Jr. (1983). *The Adjective Check List Manual-1983 Edition*. Palo Alto, CA: Consulting Psychologists Press.

Guilford, J. P. (1959). *Personality*. N. Y.: McGraw Hill.

Guilford, J. P. (1975). Factors and factors of personality. *Psychological Bulletin, 82*, 802-814.

Guilford, J. P., Guilford, J. S., & Zimmerman, W. S. (1978). *The Guilford-Zimmerman Temperament Survey manual, 1978 revision*. Beverly Hills: Sheridan Supply Company, 1978.

Guttman, L. (1950). The basis for scalogram analysis. In Stouffer, S. A., Guttman, L., Suchman, E. A., Lazarsfeld, P. A., Star, S. A., & Clausen, J. A., (Eds.), *Measurement and Prediction* (Studies in Social Psychology in World War II, Vol. 4). Princeton: Princeton University Press.

Hampson, S. E. (1982). Person memory: A semantic category model of personality traits. *British Journal of Psychology, 73*, 1-11. (a).

Hampson, S. E. (1982). *The construction of personality: An introduction*. London: Routledge and Kegan Paul. (b)

Hampson, S. E. (1983). Trait ascription and depth of acquaintance: The preference for traits in personality descriptions and its relation to target familiarity. *Journal of Research in Personality, 17*, 398-411.

Hirschberg, N. (1978). A correct treatment of traits. In H. London (Ed.), *Personality: A new look at metatheories*. Washington: Hemisphere.

Hogan, R. (1983). A socioanalytic theory of personality. In M. Page (Ed.), *Personality-Current theory and research: 1982 Nebraska Symposium on Motivation* Lincoln, NB: University of Nebraska Press.

Hogan, R. (1986). Personality psychology: Back to basics. In J. Aronoff, A. I. Rabin, & R. A. Zucker (Eds.), *The emergence of personality* (pp. 141-188). New York: Springer-Verlag.

Hogan, R., DeSoto, C., & Solano, C. (1977). Traits, tests, and personality research. *American Psychologist, 32*, 255-264.

Holden, R. R., Helmes, E., Fekken, G. C., & Jackson, D. N. (1985). The multidimensionality of person reliability: Implications for interpreting individual test item responses. *Educational and Psychological Measurement, 45*, 119-130.

Hulin, C. L., Drasgow, F., & Parsons, C. K. (1983). *Item response theory: Application to Psychological Measurement*. Homewood, IL: Dow-Jones.

Hunt, J. McV. (1936). Psychological government and the high variability of schizophrenic patients. *American Journal of Psychology, 48*, 64-81.

Jackson, D. N. (1986). The process of responding in personality assessment. In A. Angleitner & J. S. Wiggins, (Eds.), *Personality Assessment via Questionnaires: Current Issues in Theory and Measurement* (pp. 7-34). Berlin: Springer.

James, W. (1890). *Principles of Psychology (Vols. I & II)*. New York: Holt.

James, W. (1907). *Pragmatism*. London: Longmans, Green, and Co.

John, O. P., Angleitner, A., & Ostendorf, F. (1988). The lexical approach to personality: A historical review of trait taxonomic research. *European Journal of Personality, 2*, 171-203.

John, O. P., (1986). *The concept of trait breadth and its application to personality research*. colloquium presentation to the department of psychology, University of California, Berkeley, April 16, 1986.

Kelly, G. A. (1963). *A theory of personality*. New York: Norton.

Kenrick, D. T., & Braver, S. L. (1982). Personality: Idiographic and Nomothetic! A rejoinder. *Psychological Review*, *89*, 182- 186.

Kenrick, D. T., & Funder, D. C. (1988). Profiting from controversy: Lessons from the person-situation debate. *American Psychologist, 43*, 23-34.

Kenrick, D. T., & Stringfield, D. O. (1980). Personality traits and the eye of the beholder: Crossing some traditional philosophical boundaries in the search for consistency in all of the people. *Psychological Review*, *87*, 88-104.

Kiesler, D. J. (1983). The 1982 interpersonal circle: A taxonomy for complementarity in human transactions. *Psychological Review, 90*, 185-214.

Kim, J. (1967). Explanation. In P. Edwards (Ed.). *The Encyclopedia of Philosophy, Vol 3* (pp. 159-163). NY: MacMillan and Free Press.

Kluckhohn, C. & Murray, H. A. (1953). Personality formation: The determinants. In C. Kluckhohn, H. A. Murray, & D. Schneider (Eds.), *Personality in nature, society, and culture (Rev. Ed.)*. NY: Knopf.

Lamiell, J. T. (1982). The case for an idiothetic psychology of personality: A conceptual and empirical foundation. *Progress in Experimental Personality Research*, *11*, 1-64.

Lanning, K. (1986). *Consistency, Scalability, and Personality Measurement*. Doctoral dissertation, University of California. (a)

Lanning, K. (1986). Traits, trait words, and the explanation of behavior. *Theoretical and Philosophical Psychology*, 6, 108-111. (b)

Lanning, K. (1987). Some reasons for distinguishing between "non-normative response" and "irrational decision." *Journal of Psychology*, 121, 109-117.

Lanning, K. (1988). Individual differences in scalability: An alternative conception of consistency for personality theory and measurement. *Journal of Personality and Social Psychology*, *55*, 142-148.

Lanning, K. (1990). *Scalability, appropriateness, and the measurement of authoritarianism*. Paper presented at the 98th Annual APA Convention, Boston, August, 1990.

Lanning, K. & Gough, H. G. (1990). *Shared variance in the California Psychological Inventory and the California Q-set*. Manuscript submitted for publication.

Lay, C. H. (1977). Some notes on the concept of cross-situational consistency. In Magnusson, D., & Endler, N. (Eds.), *Personality at the crossroads: Current issues in interactional psychology*. Hillsdale, NJ: Erlbaum.

Leary, T. (1957). *Interpersonal diagnosis of personality*. New York: Ronald.

Lewin, K. (1951). *Field theory in social science: Selected theoretical papers*. New York: Harper.

Loevinger, J. (1957). Objective tests as instruments of psychological theory [Monograph]. *Psychological Reports*, *3*, 635-694.

Loevinger, J. (1987). *Paradigms of personality*. NY: Freeman

MacCorquodale, K. & Meehl, P. E. (1948). On a distinction between hypothetical constructs and intervening variables. *Psychological Review*, *55*, 95-107.

Magnusson, D. (1978). On the psychological situation. *Reports of the Department of Psychology, University of Stockholm*, No. 544.

Magnusson, D., & Endler, N. S. (Eds.). (1977). *Personality at the crossroads* Hillsdale, NJ: Erlbaum.

Markus, H. (1977). Self-schemata and processing information about the self. *Journal of Personality and Social Psychology, 35*, 63-78.

Markus, H., Crane, M., Bernstein, S., & Siladi, M. (1982). Self schemas and gender. *Journal of Personality and Social Psychology, 42*, 38-50.

Markus, H., Smith, J., & Moreland, R. (1985). Role of the self-concept in the perception of others. *Journal of Personality and Social Psychology, 49*, 1494-1512.

McNemar, Q. (1969). Moderation of a moderator technique. *Journal of Applied Psychology, 53*, 69-72.

McReynolds, P. (1951). Perception of Rorschach concepts as related to personality deviations. *Journal of Abnormal and Social Psychology, 46*, 131-141.

Megargee, E. I. (1972). *The California Psychological Inventory Handbook.* S.F.: Jossey-Bass.

Mellers, B. A., & Birnbaum, M. H. (1982). Loci of contextual effects in judgment. *Journal of Experimental Psychology: Human Perception and Performance, 8*, 582-601.

Mill, J. S. (1879) *A System of Logic: Ratiocinative and Inductive, being a connected view of the principles of evidence and the methods of scientific investigation, (10th edition)*. London: Longmans, Green, and Co.

Mischel, W. (1968). *Personality and assessment*. NY: Wiley.

Mischel, W. (1973). Toward a cognitive social learning reconceptualization of personality. *Psychological Review, 80*, 252 -253.

Mischel, W. (1985). *Personality: Lost or found? Identifying when individual differences make a difference*. Presidential address to Division 8 of the American Psychological Association, Los Angeles, August 25, 1985.

Mischel, W., & Peake, P. K. (1982). Beyond deja vu in the search for cross-situational consistency. *Psychological Review, 89*, 730-755.

Mitra, S. K. & Fiske, D. W. (1956). Intra-individual variability as related to test score and item. *Educational and Psychological Measurement, 16*, 3-12.

Moos, R. H. (1968). Situational analysis of a therapeutic community milieu. *Journal of Abnormal Psychology, 73*, 49-61.

Morris, J. H., Sherman, J. D., & Mansfield, E. R. (1986). Failures to detect moderating effects with ordinary least squares-moderated multiple regression: Some reasons and a remedy. *Psychological Bulletin, 99*, 282-288.

Murphy, G. (1947). *Personality: A biosocial approach to origins and structure.* NY: Basic.

Murray, H. A. et al (1938). *Explorations in Personality* Oxford: Oxford University Press.

Nisbett, R. E. & Ross, L. D. (1980). *Human inference: Strategies and shortcomings of social judgement*. Englewood Cliffs, NJ: Prentice Hall.

Norman, W. T. (1963). Toward an adequate taxonomy of personality attributes: Replicated factor structure in peer nomination personality ratings. *Journal of Abnormal and Social Psychology , 66*, 574-583.

Norman, W. T. (1969). "To see oursels as ithers see us!": Relations among self-perceptions, peer-perceptions, and expected peer-perceptions of personality attributes. *Multivariate Behavioral Research, 4*, 417-443.

Nunnally, J. C. (1978). *Psychometric theory*. (2nd Ed.). New York: McGraw-Hill.

Orford, J. (1986) The rules of interpersonal complementarity: Does hostility beget hostility and dominance, submission? *Psychological Review, 93*, 365-37

Oxford English Dictionary (1971), Compact Edition. Oxford: Oxford University Press

Ozer, D. J. (1985). Correlation and the coefficient of determination. *Psychological Bulletin*, *97*, 307-315.

Ozer, D. J. (1986). *Consistency in personality: A methodological framework*. Berlin: Springer-Verlag.

Paunonen, S. V., & Jackson, D. N. (1985). Idiographic measurement strategies for personality and prediction: Some unredeemed promissory notes. *Psychological Review*, *92*, 486-511.

Pervin, L. A. (1983). The stasis and flow of behavior. In M. Page (Ed.), *Personality-Current theory and research: 1982 Nebraska Symposium on Motivation* Lincoln, NE: University of Nebraska Press.

Petersen, P. G. (1965). *Reliability of judgments of personality as a function of subjects and traits being judged*. Unpublished doctoral dissertation, University of California, Berkeley.

Price, R. V., & Bouffard, D. L. (1974). Behavioral appropriateness and situational constraint as dimensions of social behavior. *Journal of Personality and Social Psychology*, *30*, 579-586.

Quine, W. V. (1974). *The Roots of Reference* La Salle, IL: Open Court

Rosenthal, R. (1978). Combining results of independent studies. *Psychological Bulletin*, *85*, 185-193.

Runyan, W. M. (1982). *Life histories and psychobiography*. NY: Oxford.

Rushton, J. P., Jackson, D. N., & Paunonen, S. V. (1981). Personality: Nomothetic or idiographic? A response to Kenrick and Stringfield. *Psychological Review*, *88*, 582-589.

Salmon, W. C. (1984). *Scientific explanation and the causal structure of the world*. Princeton: Princeton University Press.

Samelson, F. (1986). Authoritarianism from Berlin to Berkeley: On Social Psychology and History. *Journal of Social Issues, 42*, 191-208.

Sato, T. (1975). *The construction and interpretation of S-P tables*. Tokyo: Meiji Tokyo (in Japanese).

Saunders, D. R. (1956). Moderator variables in prediction. *Educational and Psychological Measurement*, *16*, 209-222.

Schank, R. L., & Abelson, R. (1977). *Scripts, plans, goals, and understanding*. Hillsdale, N. J.: Erlbaum.

Schneiderman, W. (1980). A personality dimension of consistency versus variability without the use of self-reports or ratings. *Journal of Personality and Social Psychology*, *39*, 158-164.

Shapiro, D. (1965). *Neurotic styles*. NY: Basic.

Shapiro, D. (1981). *Autonomy and rigid character*. NY: Basic.

Shweder, R. A. (1982). Fact and artifact in trait perception: The systematic distortion hypothesis. *Progress in Experimental Personality Research*, *2*, 65-100.

Simonton, D. K. (1989). Shakespeare's sonnets: A case of and for single-case historiometry. *Journal of Personality*, *57*, 695-721.

Skinner, B. F. (1953). *Science and Human Behavior*. NY: MacMillan.

Smith, R. M. (1986). Person fit in the Rasch model. *Educational and Psychological Measurement, 46*, 359-372.

Snyder, M. (1974). The self-monitoring of expressive behavior. *Journal of Personality and Social Psychology*, *30*, 526-537.

Stagner, R. (1933). The relation of personality to academic aptitude and achievement. *Journal of Educational Research*, *26*, 648-660.

Steffens, L. (1931). *The autobiography of Lincoln Steffens (Vol I and II)*. NY: Harcourt, Brace, & World.

Stone, E. F., & Hollenbeck, J. R. (1984). Some issues associated with the use of moderated regression. *Organizational Behavior and Human Performance, 34*, 195-213.

Stones, M. & Burt, G. (1978). Quasi-statistical inference in rating behavior-I. Preliminary investigations. *Journal of Research in Personality, 13*, 381-389.

Strelau, J. (1983). *Temperament, personality, activity.* London: Academic.

Strelau, J. (1985). Temperament and personality: Pavlov and beyond. In J. Strelau, F. H. Farley, & A. Gale (Eds.), *The biological bases of personality and behavior, Volume 1* (pp. 25-44). Washington: Hemisphere.

Stricker, L. J. (1966). Compulsivity as a moderator variable: A replication and an extension. *Journal of Applied Psychology, 50*, 331-335.

Tatsuoka, K. K. (1984). Caution indices based on Item Response Theory. *Psychometrika, 49*, 95-110.

Taylor, C. (1970). The explanation of purposive behavior. In R. Borger & F. Cioffi (Eds.), *Explanation in the Behavioural Sciences* (pp. 49-79). Cambridge: Cambridge University Press.

Taylor, R. (1967). Causation. In p. Edwards (Ed.). *The Encyclopedia of Philosophy, Vol 2* (pp. 56-66). NY: MacMillan and Free Press.

Tellegen, A. (1982). *Brief manual for the Differential Personality Questionnaire.* Unpublished manuscript, University of Minnesota.

Tellegen, A. (1988). The analysis of consistency in personality assessment. *Journal of Personality, 56*, 621-662.

Tellegen, A., Kamp, J., & Watson, D. (1982). Recognizing individual differences in predictive structure *Psychological Review, 89*, 95-105.

Thorndike, R. L. (1954). The psychological value systems of psychologists. *American Psychologist, 9*, 787-789.

Tisak, J. (1988, August). *On the stochastics of moderated multiple regression.* Paper presented at the 96th annual convention of the American Psychological Association, Atlanta, GA.

Tryon, W. W. (1979). The test-trait fallacy. *American Psychologist, 34*, 402-406.

Tukey, J. W. (1977). *Exploratory data analysis.* Reading, MA: Addison-Wesley.

Tunnell, G. (1980). Intraindividual consistency in personality assessment: The effect of self-monitoring. *Journal of Personality, 48*, 220-231.

Tupes, E. C., & Christal, R. E. (1961). *Recurrent personality factors based on trait ratings.* Technical report ASD-TR-61-97. Personnel Laboratory, Aeronautical Systems Division, Air Force Systems Command, United States Air Force. Lackland Air Force Base, Texas.

Wertheimer, M. (1945). *Productive thinking.* N.Y.: Harper.

Wiggins, J. S. (1974). *In defense of traits.* Invited address to the Ninth Annual Symposium on Recent Developments in the use of the MMPI. Los Angeles February 28, 1974

Wiggins, J. S. (1982). Circumplex models of interpersonal behavior in clinical psychology. In P.C. Kendall & J.N. Butcher (Eds.), *Handbook of research methods in clinical psychology* (pp. 183-221). New York: Wiley.

Wittgenstein, L. (1953). *Philosophical Investigations (3rd Ed., English text, G. E. M. Anscombe, Trans.)* NY: MacMillan.

Wright, B. D. (1977). Solving measurement problems with the Rasch model. *Journal of Educational Measurement, 14*, 97-116.

Zedeck, S. (1971). Problems with the use of "moderator" variables. *Psychological Bulletin, 76*, 295-310.

Zedeck, S., Cranny, C. J., Vale, C. A., and Smith, P. C. (1971) Comparison of 'joint moderators' in three prediction techniques. *Journal of Applied Psychology*, *55*, 234-240.

Zuckerman, M., Koestner, R., DeBoy, T., Garcia, T., Maresca, B. C., & Sartoris, J. M. (1988) To predict some of the people some of the time: A reexamination of the moderator variable approach in personality theory. *Journal of Personality and Social Psychology*, *54*, 1006-1019.

Appendix 1 - Situation Behavior Inventory (SBI)

Instructions

Overview In this study, you will be asked a series of questions on the computer screen. These will be presented in two sessions. The first session will be approximately 90 minutes long. The second session will be approximately 60 minutes long. During the interval in between the two sessions, you will be asked to complete several forms at home describing your moods, attitudes, and activities.

Your answers will be strictly confidential. Your responses are labelled by code number only. No information will ever be released which could identify you personally. This study has been sanctioned by the campus Committee for the Protection of Human Subjects.

At the end of the second session, you will receive three hours experimental credit. Also, several weeks after the study is completed, 'feedback' on a number of aspects of your personality will be made available to you, if you so desire.

Your responses will be used in my doctoral dissertation research, which examines several methods for trying to understand people's personalities. This research would be impossible without your participation; your cooperation is greatly appreciated.

Instructions for computer sessions. On the computer, you will encounter several types of items. The first set of items describe situations commonly encountered by University undergraduates. Read the description of the situation at the top of the screen, and think about what you would actually do, if you were in that situation. At the bottom of the screen, 18 'behaviors' are described. Then choose the behavior from the list which best matches what you would actually do, if you were in that situation.

For some situations, it may be difficult to find a behavior which matches what you would do. You should chooses the one which best matches, even if the match is not perfect. Your choice of a behavior should not be based on which behavior 'sounds right', nor should your choice be based on what people 'should do'. Instead, choose the behavior which best matches what you would really do, as you actually are. After you have made this choice, press the key with the appropriate letter (A-R). Then press the key marked RETURN.

The second set of items includes primarily 'True - False' items. Decide whether or not each statement is true, as it applies to you. Respond as you actually are, not as you feel you 'should be' or 'would like to be'. Press T or F, then RETURN.

If you make a mistake, press the BACK SPACE or left arrow (<-) key to change your answer.

If you have any questions, please raise your hand and the investigator will assist you.

Items

1. Someone scratches one of your phonograph records.
2. The garbage needs to be taken out, but it is someone else's responsibility.
3. You are with some friends who are planning to do something which you feel is wrong or inappropriate.
4. A student needs someone to spend an hour being a research subject and asks if you will participate. But you think you may not be appropriate for the experiment.
5. The apartment manager or landlord refuses to fix the leak in your kitchen sink.
6. A friend asks you to drive him or her to the city to do some shopping.
7. You are traveling or backpacking with a friend who has been complaining about the load. You told him or her when you left to pack lightly, but the person didn't listen.
8. There is a lecture you want to attend at the same time as a study group some friends have scheduled.
9. You need to get your homework done. A friend asks if you want to work with him or her.
10. You have been working on a difficult homework problem all day.
11. You just finished taking your first final exam of the semester; you think you did extremely well.
12. You are just drifting off to sleep, when your roommate gets home with some friends.
13. Two other students need a pencil for a computer-scored test, you have one extra.
14. Other people are in the kitchen while you are preparing a meal, but no one offers to help cook.
15. You think you might have an infection.
16. You are helping your friend with errands; your friend is taking a long time.
17. A friend is supposed to call but doesn't.
18. An upcoming competition offers the possibility of advancement but you are not sure if you will do well or adequately.
19. All your friends are going to the football game, but you have an exam on Monday.
20. You have a date, but your father says that you can't go out.
21. Your parents tell their friends that you are interested in their son or daughter.
22. It is late at night and a stranger is waiting outside your apartment building or dorm for someone to open the door.
23. You don't really have any questions but when you walk by your favorite professor's office during office hours, there are no other students in the room.
24. Someone in whom you are interested sits down at your table at dinner while your friends are laughing loudly and playing around.

25. You see a friend with whom you have recently had an upsetting misunderstanding.
26. You are working on a project with another student; the student makes a mistake and lets people believe that it was your fault.
27. You are almost finished with a homework problem, but you should leave now if you are going to arrive at your appointment on time.
28. You help a neighbor with homework at the neighbor's request, but then the person acts like you are flirting with him or her.
29. The instructor or assistant loses your best paper and doesn't even believe that you completed the assignment.
30. Somebody tries to sneak in line ahead of you in the administration building.
31. You can't find your notes for your hardest class; it looks as though they may be lost.
32. The instructor or teaching assistant gives you an unfair lab grade.
33. A friend has a birthday party a few days before finals.
34. A man asks you for money for coffee.
35. As you are heading off to class, you realize that your car has a flat tire.
36. A friend asks to 'look at' the math or science homework that you have just completed.
37. You are caught up in all but one of your classes and have no obligations today. A friend calls up and asks what you feel like doing.
38. On the telephone, your mother is asking you a lot of questions about your personal life.
39. Your friend acts mad at you, but won't tell you why.
40. You are riding your bicycle and people bother or harass you.
41. You land at the airport and are deciding how to get home.
42. Someone close to you seems really upset about something and is arguing with you to let off steam.
43. You are spending the night at a friends' house. Everyone is planning to attend religious services the next morning.
44. A parent or authority figure talks to you in an accusatory tone.
45. You haven't taken good notes and the exam is coming up.
46. You are trying to study at the library but it is too noisy.
47. A person hints about getting a ride home but it would be a long detour for you.
48. It is stormy out; you are studying at home. You have a seminar that meets shortly and are deciding whether or not to attend.
49. You are at a party where there is a person to whom you are attracted.
50. An acquaintance asks to borrow your registration card in order to go swimming on campus.
51. A friend says that you cheated in a game and you didn't.
52. An instructor makes your life difficult.
53. The stereo breaks and no one else takes responsibility.
54. The house is out of food and everybody is deciding who will shop.
55. You are torn between finishing a paper and having your boyfriend or girlfriend visit.
56. You need money for art supplies.
57. A good friend of yours is performing for the first time and needs support, but you have to prepare for an exam.
58. You are looking at an attractive person of the opposite sex and the person looks back at you.

59. You stayed up late last night studying. The alarm goes off but you are still tired.
60. Your friend shows up an hour late for a date.
61. You are disappointed because you got a poor grade after working hard on a paper. A friend who barely worked and got an A asks if you want to 'celebrate'.
62. An instructor asks you to come by his or her office; when you get there, he or she only wants the phone number of another student.
63. A friend throws ice down your shirt.
64. Two of your close friends are visiting; they get into an argument with each other.
65. In a seminar, another student contradicts you but you are sure that you are right.
66. You have an important exam coming up. A friend who is confused about the material asks you for help.
67. You thought you had written a good paper, but, when it is returned to you, it has insulting comments as well as a poor grade.
68. You don't like your new haircut.
69. Some friends are having difficulties. You are discussing this with another friend, but this friend doesn't appreciate the gravity or seriousness of the situation.
70. The instructor 'corrects' your spelling on a paper, but according to the dictionary, your spelling is acceptable.
71. Someone you showed an interest in last year is talking with your friends.
72. You and your roommates are going to have a party but they aren't helping in the preparations.
73. You and another student had agreed to each summarize half of the readings for a class that you take together. You are supposed to meet to exchange notes the next day, but you haven't yet done the work.
74. You need to do your Computer Science homework, but the computer has been 'down' for hours.
75. Everyone is watching football at a friend's house but you feel like you should be studying.
76. Just as you are turning in your homework assignment, you find a minor error that had been overlooked.
77. Your boyfriend or girlfriend calls up after not calling for several days, but then discusses only homework.
78. You stumble on the steps in the lecture hall.
79. You know the answer in foreign language class but you feel uncomfortable with your accent.
80. In a study group, everyone needs help with an area that you understand well, but you have questions about the rest of the material.
81. A friend is helping you with homework and says something flirtatious.
82. You go to a movie, but upon arriving at the theater you realize that you don't have enough money for a ticket.
83. You are discussing business with someone that owes you money.
84. You should finish studying, but you are getting sleepy.
85. A friend is scared by an insect or small animal.
86. For no reason, the instructor says that you cheated on the exam.
87. Your friend is sick and can't fulfill his or her responsibilities at a meeting tonight.
88. A friend calls while you are studying and is upset or concerned.
89. You run out of paper while typing your English assignment.
90. One of your housemates has been on the phone for over an hour and you are hoping or waiting for a call.

91. Your roommate wants to watch television, but it would be disruptive and you want to study.
92. Your parents want you to attend a family gathering but you have made other plans.
93. An acquaintance asks to borrow money because his or her automatic teller isn't working and the bank is closed.
94. You have just completed most of the work on a term paper, and are somewhat tired. Some friends call and ask if you want to get together with them.
95. You are supposed to attend a meeting, but have your own work as well.
96. You have a chance to work and make extra money at the same time that you had hoped to spend with your friend.
97. Your roommates are noisy during finals week.
98. Someone who you hadn't thought about a great deal expresses a romantic interest in you.
99. Late at night, you are at home studying. An acquaintance calls to ask you to drive him or her to a friend's house.
100. It is your first time in the exercise class or weight room.
101. At a meeting, they need a volunteer and no one is answering.
102. You were invited to dinner at a friend's house, but you don't have a car and the friend lives several miles away.

SBI Scale composition: Non-extreme scales

Achievement: All items except for numbers 18 32 41 54 65 73 76 95
Conscientiousness: All items except for numbers 6 36 65 66 73 76 88 95
Friendliness: All items except for numbers 6 13 26 36 37 46 50 54 66 80 87 88
Irritability: All items except for numbers 6 11 13 33 36 37 42 47 50 57 66 71 80 81 85 87 88 93 94
Self-consciousness: All items except for numbers 1 2 4 11 12 14 22 28 30 32 34 42 60 63 70 72 81 83 90 97 99 101 102

Appendix 2 - Programs for computing scalability

Pascal program for VM/CMS

```
Program residual (rawfl, rowfl, colfl, residfl);

        {1986 - The present version of program runs under vm/cms on an ibm 30xx
        or 43xx mainframe. Elimination of screen routines will allow
        the program to run under standard pascal. 1990 - A simpler SAS
        routine is also available.}
Const
  nrow    = 204; {number of persons or rows in matrix}
  ncol    =  30; {number of situs or columns}
  missing =   0; {missing values specifier}
  inprlin =   8; {number of variables per line in input file}
  inwidth =   8; {width of input vars}
Type
  matrix  = array  1..nrow,1..ncol  of integer;
  rowvec  = array  1..nrow  of integer;
  colvec  = array  1..ncol  of integer;
  idarray = array  73..80, 1..nrow  of char;
Var
  row, col, recnum, index , grnmean, loc          : integer;
  coleff, okcol, sumcolef, residcol               : colvec;
  roweff, okrow, sumrowef, residrow               : rowvec;
  averow,avecol, sumrow,sumcol                    : real;
  raw, pred, resid                                : matrix;
  rawfl, rowfl, colfl, residfl, ttyout            : text;
  alpha                                           : char;
  id                                              : idarray;
Procedure reading  (row, col, index :integer; var id: idarray; var rawfl : text);
        begin {procedure}
          for row := 1 to nrow do
          begin
                for col := 1 to ncol do
                begin
                      read (rawfl, raw row,col );
                      if (col = ncol) then
                      begin
                            loc := (inwidth * (col mod inprlin)) + 1;
                            if loc = 1 then loc := (inprlin * inwidth) + 1;
                            for index := loc to 72 do read (rawfl, alpha);
                            for index := 73  to 80 do
                                          read (rawfl, id  index,row );
                            readln (rawfl);
                      end
```

```
                                else
                                if col mod inprlin = 0 then readln (rawfl);
                        end; {col}
            end;  {row}
          end; {procedure}
Procedure coleffec (row, col : integer; var raw : matrix);
          begin {procedure}
            for col :=1 to ncol do
            begin
                    sumcolef col  := 0;
                    okcol col   := 0;
                    for row := 1 to nrow do
                    if  (raw row,col  {} missing) then
                    begin
                      sumcolef col := sumcolef col  + raw row,col ;
                      okcol col  :=okcol col  + 1;
                    end;  {adding non missing or o.k. data}
                    if okcol col  {} 0 then
                      coleff col  := round (sumcolef col /okcol col )
                    else
                    begin
                      coleff col  := 9999;
                      writeln (ttyout, 'no valid data for col ',col);
                    end;{missing}
            end; {col }
          end; {procedure}
Procedure roweffec (row, col : integer; var raw : matrix);
          begin {procedure}
            for row :=1 to nrow do
            begin
                    sumrowef row  := 0;
                    okrow row   := 0;
                    for col := 1 to ncol do
                    if  (raw row,col  {} missing) then
                    begin
                      sumrowef row := sumrowef row  + raw row,col ;
                      okrow row  :=okrow row  + 1;
                    end;  {adding non missing or o.k. data}
                    if okrow row  {} 0 then
                      roweff row  := round (sumrowef row /okrow row )
                    else
                    begin
                      roweff row  := 9999;
                      writeln (ttyout, 'no valid data for row ',row);
                    end; {missing}
            end; {row }
          end; {procedure}
Procedure granmean (row, col, index: integer; var grnmean: integer);
 begin
          sumrow := 0;
          sumcol := 0;
```

```
          index := 0;
          for row := 1 to nrow do
            begin
                    if roweff  row  {} 9999 then
                    begin
                     sumrow := sumrow + roweff row ;
                     index := index + 1
                    end;
            end;
          averow := round (sumrow / index);
          index := 0 ;
          for col := 1 to ncol do
            begin
                    if coleff  col  {} 9999 then
                    begin
                      sumcol := sumcol + coleff col ;
                      index := index + 1
                    end;
            end;
          avecol := round (sumcol / index);
          for index:= 1 to 3 do writeln (ttyout);
          writeln (ttyout,
            'average row = ', averow:4,'. average col= ',avecol:4,'.');
          for index:= 1 to 3 do writeln (ttyout);
          grnmean := round ((averow + avecol)/ 2);
  end; {procedure}
Procedure residual (row, col, grnmean: integer; var resid: matrix);
          begin {procedure}
            for row := 1 to nrow do
            begin
                    for col := 1 to ncol do
                    begin
                     if raw   row,col  = missing then
                               pred  row,col  := missing
                     else
                     begin
                              pred row,col  := (roweff row  + coleff col  - grnmean);
                              resid row,col  :=  abs (raw row,col  - pred  row,col ) ;
                     end; { else }
                    end; { col }
            end;  { row }
           end;  {procedure}
Procedure writing (row, col, index: integer; id : idarray; var residfl, rowfl, colfl : text);
          begin
            for row := 1 to nrow do
            begin
                    recnum := 0;
                    for col := 1 to ncol do
                    begin
                      write (residfl,resid  row, col :8);
                      if ((col mod 8) = 0) or (col = ncol) then
```

```
                    begin
                              if (col = ncol) and (col mod 8 {} 0) then
                              begin
                                for index := (col mod 8) to 7
                                do write (residfl,'    ');
                              end; {short record loop}
                              recnum := recnum + 1;
                              write (residfl, '   res', recnum:2);
                              for index := 73 to 80 do
                                write (residfl, id index, row );
                              writeln (residfl);
                    end; {record}
          end; {col};
  end; {writing resid file}
  for col := 1 to ncol do
  begin
          residcol col  := 0;
          for row := 1 to nrow do
           residcol col  := residcol  col  + resid  row,col ;
          if okcol col  {} 0 then
           residcol col  := round (residcol  col /okcol  col )
          else
           residcol col  := 9999;
          writeln (colfl,'column =   ',col:4,' mean = ', coleff col :8,
           ' n = ',okcol col :4,
           ' ave. resid = ',residcol col :4);
  end; {writing col file}
  for row := 1 to nrow do
  begin
          residrow row  := 0;
          for col := 1 to ncol do
                  residrow row  := residrow  row  + resid  row,col ;
          if okrow row  {} 0 then
                  residrow row  := round (residrow  row /okrow  row )
          else
            residrow row  := 9999;
          write (rowfl, '         ');
          for index := 73 to 80 do
                            write (rowfl, id index, row );
          writeln (rowfl,' mean = ', roweff row :8,
                  ' n = ',okrow row :4,
                  ' ave. resid = ',residrow row :4);
  end; {writing row file}
 end; {procedure}
Begin {main program starts here}
 reset (rawfl);
 termout (ttyout);
 reading  (row, col, index, id, rawfl);
 coleffec (row, col, raw);
 roweffec (row, col, raw);
 granmean (row, col, index, grnmean);
```

```
            residual (row, col, grnmean, resid);
            rewrite  (residfl);
            rewrite  (rowfl);
            rewrite  (colfl);
            writing (row, col, index, id, residfl, rowfl, colfl);
            close (colfl);
            close (rowfl);
            close (residfl);
end.
```

SAS program: Proc matrix routine (for SAS Version 5.18 under VM/CMS)

```
Options nocenter ls = 132;
Title 'scalability analysis';
  cms filedef datain disk response data a;
Data a;
 infile datain;
 input (item formats here);
Data b;
 infile datain;
 input (id format here);
*--------------------------------------------------------
 yij:   the person by item matrix
*--------------------------------------------------------;
Proc matrix  ; * print;
 fetch yij data=a ;
 fetch name data=b ;
 npersons=nrow(yij);
 nitems  =ncol(yij);
 elev    = yij (,+);
 irow    = i(npersons);
 onerow  = j(npersons,1,1);
 icol    = i(nitems  );
 onecol  = j(nitems,1,1);
 colcent = irow - (onerow * onerow') #/ npersons;
 rowcent = icol - (onecol * onecol') #/ nitems;
 residij = colcent * yij * rowcent;
 residij = abs (residij);
 scal    = -residij (,+);
 list = name || scal || elev;
 print list format = 6.3;
End;
```

Index